The  Servant as Leader

Kent M. Keith, editor

from the original essay
by Robert K. Greenleaf

The Contemporary Servant as Leader

Kent M. Keith, Editor

The Greenleaf Center for Servant Leadership

This project was made possible
by a gift from Cheryl and Chris Bachelder.

Contents

Editor's Preface

The Servant as Leader is the first of four essays on servant leadership written by Robert K. Greenleaf. It was first published in 1970, and then revised and republished by Greenleaf in 1973. The revised edition is often referred to as *The Orange Book* because it has traditionally been published with an orange cover.

The Servant as Leader is Greenleaf's classic essay, the one that launched the modern servant leadership movement. Hundreds of thousands of copies have been sold, and it has been translated into more than a dozen languages. It is required reading in many college classrooms. Experts on leadership and management have given the essay high praise. The essay has had a life-changing impact on many people, including myself and contributors to this publication. Greenleaf's ideas continue to be immensely important.

Greenleaf worked for AT&T for thirty-eight years, from 1926 to 1964. During those years, AT&T was one of the largest corporations in the world, with more than a million employees. Greenleaf started by digging telephone poles, and gradually became involved in teaching, training, employee assessment, and management education. Toward the end of his career, he was the company's Director of Management Research. It was his job to figure out how to help the leaders and managers of one of the world's largest corporations to be as effective as possible. What he learned was that the most effective leaders were focused on serving others. He called these people servant-leaders.

Greenleaf spent his career in the world of business, and he understood the daily realities of a complex organization. After he retired, he reflected on what he had learned. Those reflections, found in his essays, are often philosophical and even abstract. It is best to read his essays slowly, and think about each paragraph. I like to read only a few pages in one sitting, in order to give his ideas time to sink in. As with all excellent thought-pieces, I see something different each time I read Greenleaf. His writings are rich and deep. They repay multiple readings.

We live in a society, however, that is accustomed to a faster pace. Some readers are not used to reading an essay that is comparatively philosophical or abstract. One purpose of this publication is to offer a version of Greenleaf's classic essay that it is easier to read. I have therefore taken the liberty of streamlining the text. I have taken another liberty, which is that I have eliminated some "thoughtful asides" that I believe are not essential to understanding the thrust of Greenleaf's message. I found it difficult to make these editorial changes because of my respect for the original essay. It is my hope that these editorial changes will make the essay more accessible and will therefore enhance its impact.

Another purpose of this publication is to demonstrate that Greenleaf's ideas are indeed "contemporary." While Greenleaf wrote his essays in the 1970s, his ideas are still fresh. He is still ahead of us, calling us to higher levels of leadership and institutional performance. Thousands of people are using Greenleaf's ideas today because his ideas move us forward.

A third purpose of this publication was to invite comments from different servant leadership experts on major sections in Greenleaf's essay. The experts were free to choose the sections they wished to address. They provided a rich variety of comments that explain what Greenleaf's ideas mean in their own lives and work. In doing so, they remind us that there is more than one "door" into Greenleaf's message, and once inside, there is more than one way to understand what one sees. I am grateful to my colleagues in the servant leadership movement—Cheryl Bachelder, Linda Belton, Pat Falotico, Don Frick, Isabel Lopez, Larry Spears, and Duane Trammell—for their insights and wisdom.

Finally, I have provided questions at the end of each section for individual reflection and group discussion. The intention is to invite you, the reader, to expand the discussion of *The Contemporary Servant as Leader* with your colleagues and friends.

—Kent M. Keith
November 2016

The Contemporary Servant as Leader

Can you be both a servant and a leader? If so, can you be effective in the real world? I think the answer to both questions is yes. The purpose of this essay is to explain why and how.

The idea of *The Servant as Leader* came to me as a result of reading a book by Herman Hesse, *Journey to the East*. It is the story of a band of men on a mythical journey. The key person in the story is Leo. He is a *servant* who does chores for the travelers, but he also lifts their morale with his positive spirit and his singing. He is the glue that holds the group together. The travelers all sense Leo's extraordinary presence.

The journey goes well until one day when Leo disappears. Without Leo, the group falls apart, and the journey has to be abandoned. They simply can't continue.

The traveler who tells the story goes looking for Leo, and after some years of wandering, he finds Leo. He discovers that Leo, whom he had known first as *servant*, was in fact the titular head of the Order that sponsored the journey. Leo is its guiding spirit, a great and noble *leader*.

You can imagine what Hesse was trying to say when he wrote this story. To me, this story clearly says that *the great leader is seen as servant first*, and that simple fact is the key to his greatness. Leo was actually the leader all of the time, but he was servant first because that was what he was, *deep down inside*. That was his true character. He was given a leadership position, but he was by nature a servant—someone who was focused on helping others. The leadership position that was given to him could be taken away. His servant nature—his desire to help others—was a part of his character, and it could not be taken away. That's why he was a servant first, a servant at heart.

§§

KENT: The last paragraph in this opening section is crucial to understanding servant leadership. Greenleaf gets our attention by taking two words that our culture defines as opposites—"servant" and "leader"—and putting them together. While the two words are tied together by a hyphen, Greenleaf makes it clear that the two words are not equal. The word "servant" is the foundational word. A servant-leader is always a servant at heart. She will be a servant at heart before, during, and after holding a leadership position, because that is who she is, *deep down inside*. The leadership position can be given or taken away, but the servant nature remains.

I recall with a smile a suggestion made by Stephen Prosser in his essay, *Servant Leadership: More Philosophy, Less Theory*. He suggested that if there is to be a theory of servant leadership, it should be a theory of servanthood, not a theory of leading. The desire to serve is the single most important characteristic that distinguishes a servant-leader from all other leaders.

He was a servant first, a servant at heart.

ISABEL: As in the case of Leo, it is easy to miss servant-leaders. They are often unseen within a group or an institution. But you clearly know when they disappear. One of the clues is how you feel around that person. I think Herman Hesse very deliberately described Leo as singing as he served. The mere thought of singing is spirit lifting; that is the essence of the serving nature of the servant-leader. People can sometimes serve and in that process diminish others. If you are more positive, more energized, more hopeful and more productive, you may be in the company of a servant-leader or a "spirit carrier" in Greenleaf's words. You feel lighter. On the other hand, if you are always exhausted when you are around that person, and end up with a negative spirit, you may be in the company of an adherent of "power over" people rather than "for" people.

DON: Why are natural servants among us so routinely overlooked? A lack of awareness and curiosity, personal grandiosity, and limiting mental models frequently get in the way of noticing the food servers, receptionists, and people of different color or income status who do their work and notice *everything*. Then there are the work colleagues (with or without fancy titles) in every organization who earn trust by being trustworthy, consistently caring about the best interests of individuals and the organization, but not writing press releases about their good deeds. These are our teachers whom we should invite to share their richness and insights.

DUANE: Early in our work teaching servant leadership at TDIndustries, we always proudly told the story of Greenleaf getting the idea of the servant-leader from the character Leo in *Journey to the East*. We would extol the virtues of Leo and present him as the archetype, a model servant-leader. Class members would

4

always nod in agreement and identify with this "hands-on, roll-up-your-shirt-sleeves, work-along-side-me" kind of leader.

And then one day, something surprising happened. A plumbing apprentice raised his hand and offered this: "I am not sure Leo was such a great servant-leader. The team he was helping or serving fell apart…disbanded. Does that mean if a servant-leader leaves a team, they can't function anymore? It would seem to me that a true servant-leader's team would continue doing good work. Perhaps Leo helped them too much."

There were defensive, contextual answers we could have given, but we saw a greater lesson from that TDPartner: the story of Leo is not meant to be dogma or doctrine but a wonderful resource for generating great dialogue about effective leadership—the kind of dialogue we had in class that day.

QUESTION: When you read the story of Leo, do any individuals come to mind—people you know who are almost unseen, but quietly serve you and others?

§§

I mention Hesse and *Journey to the East* for two reasons. First, I want to acknowledge where I got the idea of *The Servant as Leader*. Second, I want to say something about prophecy.

A few years ago I concluded that we in this country were in a leadership crisis, and that I should do whatever I could about it. I became painfully aware that I did not have much of a sense of contemporary prophecy. And I

5

have asked myself why we don't pay attention to the prophetic voices in our midst.

I believe that clear and insightful prophetic voices are speaking all of the time. Men and women as good as the greatest prophets of the past are with us now, addressing the problems of the day. They are pointing to a better way and to a way of being that allows us to live fully and serenely in these times.

Some periods of time seem to be rich in prophetic vision, and some do not. The difference is due to the response of the listeners. If people listen to the prophet, the prophet grows in stature. If people don't listen, the talent of the prophet may wither away.

It is *seekers*, then, who make the prophet—people who are searching for and responding to the voice of a contemporary prophet. We *choose* those we want to listen to as prophets—*both old and new*—and combine their advice with our own opinions. Then we test the results in real-life experiences, and establish our own position.

Some people believe that the prophets of old have given the "word" for all time, and that contemporary prophets do not speak to our condition the way the older ones do. But if one really believes that the "word" has been given for all time, how can you be a seeker? How can you hear the contemporary voice when you have decided to turn him off?

I can't prove that either choice is better, but I think the more *hopeful* choice is the one that offers a significant role in prophecy to every individual today. One cannot interact with a dead prophet, but one can interact with

Men and women as good as the greatest prophets of the past are with us now, addressing the problems of the day.

a living one. "Faith," Dean Inge has said, "is the choice of the nobler hypothesis."

I don't think we should ignore the great voices of the past. And we shouldn't wake up each morning and try to reinvent the wheel. But if you are a *servant*, either a leader or a follower, you are always searching, listening, and expecting that a better wheel is being made. It may emerge any day. Any one of us may discover it.

I am hopeful for these times, despite the tension and conflict, because more servants are trying to see the world as it is and are listening carefully to prophetic voices that are speaking *now*. They are challenging pervasive injustice with greater force. They are also challenging the gap between the quality of society they know is reasonable and possible, and the actual performance of the whole range of institutions that exist to serve society. They know that we could be doing better, even without additional resources.

§§

ISABEL: Prophetic voices are hard to hear because they challenge a belief system that people may feel they need in order to survive. The more that one relies on that belief system, the harder it is to be open to those prophetic voices that call us to pay attention. I often think that many prophetic voices call out the sin of racism in today's society—still—but the fear of what life might be without that belief system keeps people stuck.

The prophetic voice calls us to listen so that we may be transformed. Ah, and can you choose the nobler hypothesis without looking for the nobility in others? And yet, is every voice that yells out a prophetic voice? How do we know? In my mind, I would look for the one who is: (1) calling for no harm to be done to others, (2) calling for good rather than for punishment of others, and (3) calling out for justice and peace. Even though the term "prophetic" is generally used in a religious sense, I think in our current world, the prophetic voices are often from outside of religious structures. That perhaps says something.

DON: Many wonder why Greenleaf discussed prophecy in this essay. Greenleaf's son Newcomb believed his father was confronting the idea that he himself could be a prophet. He was also synthesizing ideas learned from various friends, including Rabbi Abraham Joshua Heschel, author of the 1962 book *The Prophets*, and the poet Robert Frost. Prophets speak truth to powerful people and systems, but also call us to ground ourselves in the higher, deeper, and nobler life-affirming powers of the heart.

Artists are a rich source of prophecy, serving the same function as the canary in the birdcage that coal miners carried into deep tunnels. Poisonous gases affected the birds before humans, so if the canaries died, it was time to head for the surface. Artists, like canaries, are early-warning prophets. For example, the 1913 New York Armory Show of modern artists like Picasso and Matisse shocked America. Their work presaged the end of an old, predictable order, which sure enough was soon shattered by World War I. Some of Bob Dylan's songs were prophetic for Baby Boomers.

KENT: Greenleaf reminds us that it is not enough to have prophets. People have to listen to them, and understand, and act. We need to ask today, and each day: Are we listening? Do we understand? Will we act?

LARRY: In 1975, *Friends Journal* published an article by Green-leaf titled, "On Being a Seeker in the Late Twentieth Century." In 1996, Anne Fraker and I included that essay in a posthumous collection of writings by Greenleaf titled, *Seeker and Servant.* It was in this article that Greenleaf postulated the idea of creating a Seekers Anonymous. This idea is close to my heart. As was the case with other powerful concepts addressed by Greenleaf, he wrote a total of three paragraphs on this idea which are included in that essay. He didn't say all that much about it; rather, he shared what inspiration and insight he had. I believe he did so with some hope that his ideas might be picked up by others and made real in some fashion.

> **QUESTIONS:** What prophets are you listening to? How are you responding?

§§

People are taking a fresh look at the issues of power and authority. They are learning to relate to each other in ways that are less coercive and more supportive. A new moral principle is emerging that holds that authority only deserves our allegiance if that allegiance is freely and knowingly granted to the leader by those who are being led. And that allegiance should only be granted when there is evidence that the leader is a servant.

Those who follow this principle will not casually accept the authority of today's institutions. *Rather, they will freely respond only to individuals who are chosen as leaders because they are proven and trusted as servants.* If this principle catches on, the only institutions that will succeed in the future will be those that are led by servants.

§§

LINDA: Power is the currency of the contemporary work world. Look deeply enough and we find that the root of one's leadership style, behaviors, decisions, and actions is power. In hierarchical organizations, the optic of power is the pyramid. Servant leadership is based on upending the hierarchy, inverting the pyramid. An upended pyramid is a compelling image of the redistribution of power. In servant-leader organizations, power is vested in moral authority and dispersed through the ranks. Servant-leaders exercise *power for* and *power with*, rather than *power over*. Servant-leaders are generous in offering others a *seat at the table.* Employees respond with full engagement, commitment, and creativity. Real power in organizations is the capacity generated by relationships. And relationships are the real work of an organization.

PAT: Leadership requires followership. How often do we conform to the will of coercive managers? That doesn't make them leaders; certainly not servant-leaders. When we conform, we are coping! We do what is expected, not more. But when we are led in supportive and caring ways, we put forth extraordinary effort.

DON: According to Greenleaf, life is messier—and more dangerous—if we claim the courage to live in paradox rather than take the easy way out through criticism or irony (a passive-aggressive form of criticism). Judgment and criticism are often

Servant-leaders exercise power for *and* power
with, *rather than* power over.

rooted in denial of what we do not like in ourselves. We project it onto others so we can react against *their* problems, *their* leadership choices, *their* thinking. Clarity comes from Greenleaf's emerging principle that we should only follow those who are servants. Here is a bedrock principle for making decisions about whom to promote, vote for, or simply follow. Yet, this decision should be made with humility and full awareness that we are all imperfect.

KENT: These two paragraphs by Greenleaf are profoundly provocative. We know that one way to change society for the better is to only follow servant-leaders and only support institutions that are led by servants. What if we actually did that? What if we decided that we simply won't go along with coercive power any longer? What if we established servant leadership as *the* accepted standard of leadership throughout society? What if millions of us demonstrated servant leadership in our own lives, and taught it to others—beginning with young people? Change starts somewhere. Why shouldn't it begin with us?

QUESTIONS: Are you following anyone who is *not* a servant-leader? Why? How does it feel? Are you following anyone who *is* a servant-leader? Why? How does it feel?

§§

I know it may be a long time before these trends become a major force shaping society. We are not there yet. But I see encouraging movement on the horizon.

What direction will the movement take? Much depends on whether those in the movement will come to grips with the age-old problem of how to live in a human society. Some may find it hard to not just criticize, but instead become *affirmative builders* of a better society. We don't know how many of them will seek their personal fulfillment by making the hard choices, and by undertaking the rigorous preparation that is required to build a better society. It all depends on what kind of leaders emerge and how they—and we—respond to them.

My idea that more servants should emerge as leaders, or should follow only servant-leaders, is not necessarily a popular one. After all, there are several less-demanding alternatives to choose. Some say that since society seems corrupt, we should retreat to an idyllic existence that minimizes involvement with the "system" (the "system" that makes it possible to withdraw in the first place). Then there is the idea that since the effort to reform existing institutions has not brought instant perfection, we should destroy them completely so that fresh, new, perfect ones can grow. But if existing institutions are destroyed, where will the new seed come from, and who will help the new seed to grow? The concept of the servant-leader is very different from this kind of thinking.

It is understandable that the easier alternatives would be chosen, especially by young people. It's not their fault. Education has been extended so far into the adult years that young people often don't participate in society, even though they are ready for it. Then there is the problem that education is mostly abstract and analytical. There is a preoccupation with criticism. Not much thought is given to the question: "what can *I* do about it?"

Criticism has its place, but as a total preoccupation it is sterile. In a time of crisis, like the leadership crisis we are now in, too many potential builders are busy dissecting what's wrong and expecting instant perfection. As a result, the movement so many of us want to see is set back. The danger is that we hear the analyst too much and the artist too little.

Albert Camus stands apart from the other great artists of his time, in my view. He deserves the title of *prophet* because of his unrelenting demand that each of us confront the exacting terms of his own existence. Like Sisyphus, each of us should *accept his rock and find his happiness in dealing with it.* In the last paragraph of his last published lecture, entitled "Create Dangerously," Camus demonstrates how his position relates to the servant as leader.

> One may long, as I do, for a gentler flame, a respite, a pause for musing. But perhaps there is no other peace for the artist than what he finds in the heat of combat... Great ideas, it has been said, come into the world as gently as doves. Perhaps, then, if we listen attentively, we shall hear, amid the uproar of empires and nations, a faint flutter of wings, the gently stirring of life and hope. Some will say that this hope lies in a nation, others, in a man. I believe rather that it is awakened, revived, nourished by millions of solitary individuals whose deeds and works every day negate frontiers and the crudest implications of history. As a result, there shines forth fleetingly the ever-threatened truth that

each and every man, on the foundations of his own sufferings and joys, builds for them all.

We must accept the human condition, with its sufferings and its joys, and work with its imperfections. That is the foundation upon which we can build our wholeness through adventurous creative achievement. For the person with creative potential there is no wholeness except in using it. And, as Camus explained, the going is rough and the respite is brief. It is significant that he would title his last university lecture *Create Dangerously*.

§§

DON: Greenleaf once wrote: "As a theorist, I am an idealist. As a practitioner, I am a realist." He believed in evolution, not revolution, and knew that a personal or organizational vision is just the *beginning* of transformative change, not the end product. Aristotle said that virtue is a matter of habit, and habits are hard to change, especially habits of thought. In our polarized times, the contradictions in society—and within ourselves—are often likely to be seen as issues of wrong versus right (a habit of either-or thinking) rather than as evidence of the human condition.

KENT: Greenleaf raises an issue that faces everyone who wants to make the world a better place. How do you do it? How do you achieve constructive change? Greenleaf argues that running away from society won't do it, but tearing everything down won't do it, either. We need potential builders, servant-leaders who will not sit back and criticize, but will enter the fray to do battle, engaging people and issues in order to move forward. We are imperfect, and the process is imperfect, but there is really no other choice but to engage people and start building a better future.

I have had the opportunity to lead the change process at a government agency, two universities, and two non-profit organizations. I have found that leading the change process is messy, and often painful. But I have also had the privilege to serve on teams that worked through the messiness and pain to achieve new levels of service and institutional integrity, changing lives for the better.

DON: Always, always, Greenleaf returns to the responsibility of an individual to act where and how she can: "For the person with creative potential there is no wholeness except in using it."

QUESTIONS: Do you agree that "we hear the analyst too much and the artist too little?" Why or why not?

§§

Combining the servant and leader seems dangerous. It is dangerous for the natural servant to become a leader, dangerous for the leader to be servant first, and dangerous for a follower to insist that he be led by a servant. There are safer and easier alternatives available to all three. But why take them?

As I respond to this question, I am faced with two problems. The first problem is that I did not get the notion of the servant as leader from conscious logic, moving from premise to conclusion. The idea came to me as an intuitive insight when I thought about Leo.

The second problem is that my world is full of contradictions. The idea of the servant as leader may be a contradiction. Here are more contradictions: I believe in social order, but I want the creativity that can emerge from chaos. My good society will have strong individualism but also strong communities. I see a place for elitism along with populism. I listen to the old and to the young and find myself baffled and heartened by both. Reason and intuition, each in its own way, both comfort and dismay me.

Yet, with all of these contradictions, I believe that I live with as much serenity as those who tie up the essentials of life in neat bundles of logic and consistency. I am deeply grateful to the people who are logical and consistent because some of them, out of their natures, render invaluable services for which I am not capable.

My resolution of these two problems is to offer what I have learned in the form of a series of unconnected little essays, some developed more fully than others, with the suggestion that they be read and pondered on separately within the context of this opening section.

§§

KENT: I like the fact that Greenleaf finds as much serenity with contradictory positions as a person who has everything tied up logically. His reflection calls to mind Emerson's statement that "a foolish consistency is the hobgoblin of little minds, adored by little statesmen and philosophers and divines." Greenleaf's serenity in the face of his own contradictions reminds me of *yin* and *yang* in the Chinese philosophical tradition—opposites that are actually complementary, and often interdependent, in the natural world. They may be opposites, but they go together, completing each other. They are parts of the bigger whole.

Greenleaf is open to learning from opposite viewpoints. This is very practical. We don't always have to pick one side and exclude the other side. By not choosing between contradictory positions, but including each, we can broaden our understanding and improve our ability to serve. To use Greenleaf's examples, why not listen to both the young and old? Why not be aware of the egalitarian and the elite? We may learn something important from each. We may eventually have to choose sides, but if we listen carefully enough, we may also find common ground that can bring opposites more closely together. Sometimes, we do more than find common ground—we find completely *new* ground. Through patient, respectful dialogue, a new truth emerges that neither side imagined and both can support.

LARRY: Regarding Greenleaf's focus on intuitive insight in this section of the essay, I agree that Robert Greenleaf's writings on servant leadership are to some degree about the implicit search for wholeness. Both Carl Jung's work and Myers-Briggs have a similar goal in mind. In 2010, Ralph Lewis and I published an essay titled, "Myers-Briggs and Servant-Leadership: The Servant-Leader and Personality Type." In this essay, we concluded that Robert Greenleaf's personality type was almost certainly INFP (Introverted-Intuitive-Feeling-Perceiving).

QUESTIONS: Are you open to learning from contradictory positions? Why or why not?

§§

Who Is the Servant-Leader?

The servant-leader *is* servant first—as Leo was portrayed. It begins with the natural feeling that one wants to serve, to serve *first*. Then, when the opportunity arises to serve by leading, the individual makes the conscious choice to lead. That person is sharply different from the person who starts with the desire to lead. The *leader first* may be motivated by a desire for personal power or wealth. It is still possible that he or she will decide later to serve— after becoming a leader.

The leader-first and the servant-first are two extreme types. Between them there are shadings that are part of the infinite variety of human nature. The difference between them shows itself in the care taken by the servant-first to make sure that other people's highest priority needs are being served. The best test, which is difficult to administer, is this: do those served grow as persons; do they, *while being served*, become healthier, wiser, freer, more autonomous, more likely themselves to become servants? *And*, what is the effect on the least privileged in society; will they benefit, or, at least, not be further deprived?

§§

What is the effect on the least privileged in society?

KENT: These two paragraphs changed my life. They have given me an ethical, practical, and meaningful framework for leading—and for thinking about leadership—during the past twenty-five years.

As a teenager, I had rejected what I call the power model of leadership, but I did not have a good way of defining "people-centered" leadership that was based on one's love for others. When I read Greenleaf's definition of the servant-leader, lights flashed, bells rang, and I knew I had found the definition I was looking for. Servant leadership starts with the desire to serve. When you see the opportunity to serve *by leading*, you assume the responsibilities of leadership. As a servant-leader, you pay attention to others, and make sure that their highest priority needs are being served. You identify and meet the needs of others, whether they are your colleagues or your customers. And you'll know you are heading in the right direction if the people you serve are growing. And yes: don't forget the least privileged. Help them if you can, but at a minimum, don't make things worse for them.

LARRY: My own introduction to servant leadership and Robert Greenleaf first came in 1982, when I was on the staff of *Friends Journal*, a Quaker magazine in Philadelphia. We received an article submission from Robert Greenleaf, which we eventually published. All these years later, I still recall my delight in seeing the word, servant-leader, and reading Greenleaf's description of its meaning. Like many others whom I have met since that time, in that moment I felt like I had discovered a vocabulary for something that I yearned to be, but that I had not been able to put into words.

ISABEL: In teaching the "Foundations of Servant Leadership" class for the Greenleaf Center, I often quote Georgia Heard's book, *Writing Toward Home*. She talks about *querencia*. She describes it as being the place from which one's strength of character is drawn. It is a place of power, a place of home.

This concept often resonates with those learning about the servant as leader. Often they say, "now I have words," or "this feels like home to me." I think this is because when Greenleaf lays out his philosophy, we sense that it is a better way, and we know this in the deepest recesses of our soul. Surely we should serve others; surely those that serve are those who should be followed as leaders for they are the ones who can be trusted with our humanity. How much better that would be rather than striving to survive under the leadership of "petty tyrants," something that most people working in institutions have experienced? I also think that Greenleaf was one of those unsung prophets who to this day is singing a song that remains vibrant and current. And surely each of us has a responsibility to be one of those servants as leaders.

CHERYL: The Servant First motto could well be "it's all about the people": others-focused leadership. This leader is in a position of power, but uses the position to share power—listening to people, collaborating with people, and seeking a win for the people and the enterprise.

PAT: Can you be a servant-leader and be soft on results? I don't think so. If we are committed to helping others meet their highest priority needs, we must make sure that the organization we lead achieves its objectives. Institutions become irrelevant if they don't fulfill their missions. That puts people at risk.

LINDA: A comment on the "least privileged" in the best test: Who are they in our organizations? Are they literally those who lack food or shelter? Or can it refer to those who are "poor in power"? In the workplace, the "least privileged" may be the employees at the bottom of the hierarchical ladder; those who have no voice; those with less education or fewer skills. It can also include the consumer of the organization's service, especially those who may be vulnerable or dependent. Whether through training, advocacy, or attentiveness to the impact of decisions and policies, the servant-leader identifies the "least privileged" and seeks opportunities to elevate them.

DON: Greenleaf's definition and "best test" of a servant-leader are the most-quoted portions of this historic essay. These few paragraphs are worthy of repeated reflection, just like Robert Frost's poem "Directive." When Greenleaf asked Frost for context to understand the poem, Frost said, "read it and read it and read it and it means what it says to you." Here are three suggestions for your reading.

First, here is a way to quickly move the definition of a servant-leader from the head to the heart and gut. Think of someone in your life who has *your* best interests at heart—a parent, religious leader, coach, work colleague, or simply a friend. He or she may sometimes be tough when calling you to accountability but you trust that this valued person will listen—really listen—and encourage your emergence into full potential. This is the servant-leader who already lives in your heart and gut, the one who is servant first—probably not always sentimental but reliably authentic.

Second, Greenleaf's advice on knowing how to serve echoes the scientific method that begins with a hypothesis, followed by study, research, action, then evaluation of the results. Results inform future hypotheses and actions in an expanding spiral of service. This is a radically different approach than following an unchanging "recipe" for servanthood which, Greenleaf would say, is not very effective and, besides, is not much fun. Greenleaf, a Quaker, uses the word *experimentally* as a way of approaching servanthood from the *inside out* to the world and from the *outside in*, down to the deepest personal and cosmic dynamics.

Third, notice that the best test for a servant-leader is not about good intentions or *outputs* like written reports, but about *outcomes*, as measured by the concrete impact servants have on those being served. It is a grounded, pragmatic test that can be verified, and researchers around the world have been doing just that. Study after study shows positive correlations between servant-leader behaviors (and servant-led organizational cultures) with markers like overall health, innovation, employee retention and satisfaction, job dedication, individual initiative, accelerated learning in the classroom and on the job and, yes, even profits. There is nothing "soft" or mysterious about why people who feel valued grow, blossom, contribute, and learn to serve others. My grandma Pearl would call it common sense.

DUANE: One passage in this section has especially helped me and many students in our servant leadership classes understand the definition of a servant-leader: "The leader-first and the servant-first are two extreme types. Between them there are shadings that are part of the infinite variety of human nature."

Early on in our work, we had a diagram with "non-servant" on one side and "servant-leader" on the other side. And as many other practitioners have done, we asked participants to fill in the chart with behaviors and traits of each type of leader. Unintentionally, we set up the idea that there are two kinds of leaders—servant-leaders and the other kind, bad leaders. Servant-leaders

= good; other kinds of leaders = bad. And most people saw themselves in the "good" category and told stories about bad bosses who were on the other side of the chart.

After a few years, we realized our good intentions were misguided. We changed the focus of this learning activity to describing "what my leadership looks like on a bad day, when I am overworked, facing deadlines, not feeling well, etc." and on the other side of the chart "what my leadership looks like on my best days." Our dialogue completely changed. People realized that we all have the capacity to be servant-leaders. We are not likely to be the best servant-leader nor are we likely to be the worst non-servant. We live in the "shadings." I love this quote from Jack Lowe, Chairman of TDIndustries: "We have been at this for seventy years, and we haven't produced a perfect servant-leader yet."

QUESTIONS: Greenleaf said that "it begins with the natural feeling that one wants to serve." Do you think that most people have that feeling? If so, where does the feeling come from? Greenleaf also said that the best test of servant leadership is: Do those served grow as persons? Why is that the best test?

§§

When you set out to serve, how can you know that you will succeed in truly serving? This is part of the human dilemma—you can't know for sure. You can come up with your own hypothesis after study and experience. Then you can act on your hypothesis and examine the results. After examining the results, you may want to re-examine the hypothesis itself. Then you choose again.

It is always a fresh choice, and you should always have some doubts about your hypothesis. "Faith is the choice of the nobler hypothesis." Not the *noblest*, because you never know what that is. But the *nobler*, the best you can see when you make a choice. Since it will take time before you will know the results of your actions, you will need faith to sustain your choice of the nobler hypothesis. The natural servant, the person who is *servant first*, perseveres and continually refines his or her hypothesis on what serves another's highest priority needs.

My hope for the future rests in part on my belief that among the legions of deprived people are many true servants who will lead, and that most of them can learn to identify the true servants.

§§

ISABEL: If I were to set up an equation for serving it would be S = S. Serving equals serving. Simple. If serving equals status, money, or recognition (even though those things might come), the serving can become tainted. In that case the equation would be S = R, serving = recognition. I think this sounds tough. Do not blame me—tell Greenleaf, again gently demanding so that we rise to become better. We are called to answer the questions, "who am I? And so what?" I like old sayings. This one seems to fit here: he who feels punctured must have once been a balloon. This is a check on our ego as we serve.

28

And are others better because we are around—as his best test asks us? Probably sometimes "yes" and sometimes "no." This I do know, others are always better off than if we were never trying to meet the best test. And as long as the best test is our guide, when we stumble or perhaps even fail, we are more apt to be forgiven because we are human. In that circle of learning, we ourselves also become better—in all ways.

KENT: I agree. If you have the desire to serve, and spend time listening to people to find out what they need, you are far more likely to truly serve than leaders who don't listen and don't care about anyone other than themselves.

PAT: When I was a young executive, I learned what being decisive really meant. The leader must use information available, weigh risks and rewards, understand the implications the decisions would have on the people involved and then *choose*. Regardless of our egos, we are never sure that the way forward is the one and only right way to proceed. All we know is that our way forward is the best alternative that we can conceive. It seems to me that bringing others into the dialog can only help us in choosing the nobler hypothesis.

> **QUESTIONS:** As Greenleaf asked, "when you set out to serve, how can you know that you will succeed in truly serving?" What kind of intentions, feedback, and results would satisfy you?

§§

Everything Begins with the Initiative of an Individual

The forces for good and evil in the world are propelled by the thoughts, attitudes, and actions of individual beings. What happens to our values, and therefore to the quality of our civilization in the future, will be shaped by the ideas of inspired individuals. Perhaps only a few will be inspired, and the rest of us will learn from them.

Leadership arises when the leader is open to inspiration. Why would anybody accept the leadership of another except that the other sees more clearly where it is best to go? Perhaps this is the current problem: too many who want to lead do not see more clearly. In defense of their inadequacy, they argue that the "system" must be preserved—a fatal error in this day of candor.

But the leader needs more than inspiration. She says, "I will go; come with me!" She initiates, provides the ideas and the structure, and takes the risk of failure along with the chance of success. She says, "I will go, follow me!" She says that even when the path is uncertain, even dangerous. And she trusts those who go with her.

Paul Goodman, speaking through a character in *Making Do* has said, "If there is no community for you, young man, young man, make it yourself."

§§

KENT: It is very hard in today's world for anyone to accomplish anything alone. And yet, a new idea, a new practice, a new vision, usually comes from an individual. It has to start somewhere! As that individual inspires others, the team can grow and become a movement, and then social change occurs.

Greenleaf is well aware that inspiration is not enough. Leaders have to have the courage to get out in front and risk failure. It is this combination of inspiration and courage that attracts followers. Who wants to follow someone who has no vision and no courage? Leadership is about sticking your neck out.

LINDA: The role of courage in servant leadership cannot be overstated. The leader who says, "I will go; follow me," even when the path is uncertain or dangerous, is a person of considerable courage. Courage is required to delegate, yet retain accountability; to step out into the unknown with less than perfect information; to accept that a community of people is relying on one's judgment and competence. It takes courage to hover in the background, nudging others into the limelight; to admit an error; to ask forgiveness; to risk failure. Critics who define servant leadership as weak and indecisive couldn't be more wrong. The quiet courage that displays compassion, trust, and mercy can move mountains. And in this courage, the servant-leader inspires others to serve by taking up the mantle of leadership themselves.

DON: In spite of pervasive cynicism that our lives are controlled by the "system," the rich, elite, or even a malevolent conspiracy, deep down we each know that for good or ill, individual acts reverberate throughout human lives and systems in unforeseen ways. That was true of Malala Yousafzai, the 14-year-old Pakistani girl who was shot on a school bus by the Taliban because

Leaders have to have the courage to get out in front and risk failure.

she defied their ban on education for girls. It was true of Mother (now Saint) Teresa of Calcutta whose care for the poor, sick, and dying blossomed into a Catholic order and a moral beacon. It is also true for you as you act as a serving parent, volunteer, and employee.

Servant leadership is not just another theory of leading; it is an *ethical* philosophy of leadership. Leaders are not necessarily ethical. They can inspire followers with a warped vision that appeals to followers' darkest corners of fear and anger. Hitler did it. Or, they may start with good intentions and become corrupted by the intoxications of power and grandiosity. All of us are susceptible to these ancient human failings, but Greenleaf believed that servant-leaders could counter them with inner disciplines that grounded the inner psyche in humility and contact with a transcendent dynamic of servanthood.

QUESTIONS: Are you open to inspiration? As a leader, are you willing to take the risk of failure along with the chance of success? Why or why not?

§§

What Are You Trying to Do?

What are you trying to do? That's an easy question to ask, but a difficult one to answer.

A leader is better than most at pointing the way. As long as he is leading, he always has a goal. It may be a goal arrived at by group consensus; or it may be that the leader, acting on inspiration, said, "let's go this way." By clearly stating and restating the goal, the leader gives certainty and purpose to others who may have difficulty in achieving it for themselves.

The word *goal* is used here in the special sense of the overarching purpose, the big dream, the visionary concept, the ultimate consummation which one approaches but never really achieves. It is something presently out of reach; it is something to strive for, to move toward, or become. It is stated in a way that excites the imagination and challenges people to work for something they do not yet know how to do—something they can be proud of as they move toward it.

Every achievement starts with a goal. But not just any goal, and not just anybody stating it. The leader who states the goal must be trusted by others, especially if it is a high risk or visionary goal, because those who follow are asked to accept the risk along with the leader. A leader does not gain the trust of others unless (1) they have confidence in her values and her competence (including judgment), and (2) she has a sustaining spirit that will support the tenacious pursuit of a goal.

Not much happens without a dream. And for something great to happen, there must be a great dream. Behind every great achievement is a dreamer of great dreams. Much more than a dreamer is required to bring it to reality; but the dream must be there first.

§§

DON: Here, Greenleaf uses the word *goal* to include "the big dream" and "visionary purpose." He is not referring to seven or ten steps of goal setting. Those are management functions. "Nothing much happens without a dream" he says, but that dream must be repeated and modeled and rooted in the heads and hearts of both leader and follower.

LINDA: Great leaders have great dreams. While the rest of us admire the dream, our natural reticence about what is practical and achievable may hold us back. Without firm conviction and confidence in a charismatic leader, we linger uncertainly on the fringes of the dream.

Charisma is defined as a personal magic that arouses special loyalty and enthusiasm. We have many historical and contemporary examples of iconic, charismatic leaders: some moved the world to righteousness; others left the world in stunning disarray. The charismatic leader can stir followers to fulfill his agenda, which is unquestionably in the best interest of the leader, and potentially in the best interest of the organization. But is it in the best interest of the followers or those being served?

I believe a servant-leader is more concerned about *charism* than *charisma*. Charism is an extraordinary power, virtue, or value which is used for the good of an organization or community.

Charisma—the ability to persuade and inspire—is at its peak when motivated by a deeply held charism. The servant-leader builds the dream on the best interests of individuals as well as the organization. By instilling a sense of collective ownership, he invites the work community to enter into the dream.

KENT: In his essay, *The Leadership Crisis*, Greenleaf wrote about the dream or the great idea as the unifying factor. "It is the *idea* that unites people in the common effort, not the charisma of the leader," he wrote. The role of the leader is to serve the dream. When the leader has faith in the dream, others will join in, and move the organization toward the accomplishment of the dream. I love this idea. It's not about the leader, it's about the dream that brings everyone together.

ISABEL: The first thing that strikes me about this passage is its call. Then I am struck by the complexity of the thinking. Then I am struck by the thought—yes, we can do this. If I think it through and want to draw a map so I can follow it, this is what I would draw.

Dream a big dream

↓

Point the way
Provide purpose and imagination
Be of sustaining and trustworthy spirit

↓

Pursue tenaciously
Share achievements we are proud of as we move
toward dream

Ahh, now I get it! Now the complex *seems* simple. But each word is layered and as we work with this idea, we unlayer it for ourselves—it has to be our own big dream. We need to develop ourselves to *be* and then we start to get there. Back to simple. Then back to complex—a dream without a sense of purpose will not hold us in good stead. Ahh, Greenleaf—ever the challenger.

QUESTIONS: Do you have a great dream? If so, what can you do to move toward the fulfillment of your dream?

§§

Listening and Understanding

A very able leader recently became the head of a large, important, public institution. After a short time he realized that he was not happy with the way things were going. He took a unique approach. For three months he stopped reading newspapers and listening to news broadcasts. Instead, he relied wholly upon the people he met in the course of his work to tell him what was going on. In three months his administrative problems were resolved. There were no miracles. It's just that he listened, and as a result, he learned a lot and gained the insights that he needed to set the right course. He also strengthened his team.

Why is there so little listening? What makes this example so exceptional? Part of it, I believe, is that a leader who faces a problem tends to react by trying to find someone else on whom to pin the problem. Instead, his automatic response should be, "I have a problem. What is it? What can *I* do about *my* problem?" The leader who takes this approach will probably react by listening, and somebody in the situation is likely to tell him what his problem is and what he should do about it. Or, he will hear enough that he will get an intuitive insight that resolves it.

I have a bias about this which suggests that only a true natural servant automatically responds to any problem by listening *first*. When she is a leader, this disposition

*Only a true natural servant automatically responds
to any problem by listening first.*

causes her to be *seen* as servant first. This suggests that someone who wants to be a servant might become a *natural* servant by learning to listen. I have seen remarkable transformations in people who have been trained to listen. It is because true listening builds strength in other people.

Most of us would really like to communicate, really connect in a meaningful way with those who hear us. It can be terribly important. The best test of whether we are communicating at this depth is to ask ourselves, first, are we really listening? Are we listening to those we want to communicate with? Is our basic attitude one of wanting to understand? Remember that great line from the prayer of St. Francis, "Lord, grant that I may not seek so much to be understood as to understand."

We should not be afraid of a little silence. Some people find silence to be awkward. Why? A relaxed approach to dialogue will include the welcoming of some silence. It is sometimes important to ask—"In saying what I have in mind will I really improve on the silence?" If the answer is no, shouldn't I be quiet, and welcome the silence?

§§

PAT: I am holding myself to a new standard: Will I improve upon the silence by saying what I have on my mind? Am I talking when I should be listening? Am I filling an awkward silence and depriving others of the space they need to arrive at their own breakthroughs? Am I speaking to get recognized for my gifts? None of those motivations help others to grow.

LINDA: Listening is a strategic advantage to the servant-leader, never more so than in today's cacophonous world of work. With so many aural images bombarding us, listening judiciously can help the leader tune out the extraneous and ferret out the essential. Wisdom often comes in whispers.

I am reminded of an exercise in which the participants are instructed to speak for one minute on any topic, then to maintain silence for thirty seconds. Staying quiet for half a minute is often deemed harder than talking extemporaneously. The body language itself speaks volumes about the degree of discomfort the participants experience.

Why are we so uncomfortable with silence? Perhaps because we expect our leaders to always have something profound to say. Maybe because silence implies hesitation or indecision. Possibly because the chatter hides a sense of inadequacy or spares us from digging deeper. We are often so concerned about getting our own points across that we don't provide a space for others to convey theirs.

There is a difference between listening discriminately and listening selectively. I recall a well-respected leader who listened attentively to managers and professionals, but tended to sift out the comments and concerns of rank and file staff. When she became aware of this inclination, she discovered what a wealth of information she had been missing.

Among all the descriptions of this servant-leader characteristic, the most provocative is this: *listening is a healing attitude.* What an empowering idea! In whatever environment the leader leads, she is called to be a *healer;* to heal systems, organizations, and employees who have been treated as commodities. That I, as a leader, might fulfill this commitment through simple, authentic listening is revelatory.

ISABEL: I like the fact that Greenleaf thought of listening as transformational. You can be transformed by really listening. So on a personal level that means not analyzing the experience of others. Just because they may not be *your* experiences does not mean they are not true. It just means that they are outside of your experience. Listening then allows for the transformation. It means: "do not judge until you have walked a mile in another's shoes." Unless you have done so, the only way you can serve well and ethically is through the active process of listening.

I remember once doing some work for a foundation that was gathering information on educational systems. We gathered a multi-ethnic group of participants to share their educational experiences. These were adults from various professions. They shared their educational stories. I was surprised when we talked later about what we learned. Several comments were made such as, "they must have heard the teacher wrong," or "I do not understand how that can be true." In other words, what was heard was foreign to their own experience and could only be analyzed as less than "truth." I know that when experiences are discounted, we do not learn from them, and others quit sharing them. Then we are all poorer and our decisions and actions are of lower quality.

Institutionally, listening allows for a broader range of thinking, experience, and knowledge to be brought to bear on problem solving. We are each limited by our own thoughts, knowledge, and experience and can only solve problems from that base. Often by using only our own base, we can make problems larger and more intractable. Then we are puzzled as to why we seem to be "solving" the same problems over and over.

KENT: Greenleaf said that listening is the premier skill of the servant-leader. That makes sense. How do you know what people need if you don't ask and then listen? Listening up front can save a lot of time later. If you don't listen, you may not understand what needs to be done, and you may do the wrong thing.

When I was appointed to the presidency of a university many years ago, I was under pressure to immediately make grand public statements about new directions, or a shake-up on campus, or bold new visions for the university's future. I frustrated a lot of reporters, and even some Board members, by refraining from making any grand statements. How could I know what to say or do before connecting with the faculty and staff? I had read what Greenleaf said about listening, so instead of making grand public statements, I started by sitting down with about thirty faculty and staff members, one-on-one, to listen to their view of the institution and its future. Then I convened a task force to develop an Action Plan for the next three years. The task force included faculty leaders, staff members, and board members. The Action Plan that we adopted was a result of studying our situation and listening to each other. Over the next three years we were able to implement the plan and greatly improve the university's position. Proclamations can be inappropriate because they are simply off base, and because they generate resistance or even backlash. By contrast, listening is respectful of others, makes it possible to build on strengths, and can bring people together in a common cause.

DON: Listening, as Greenleaf defines it, goes beyond the tips and tricks of "active listening" you can look up on the internet. It involves a heightened sense of awareness of verbal and body language and a feel for emotional dynamics, but mostly requires personal *presence* by the listener. This kind of listening not only changes the speaker but also the listener, who is open to understanding rather than planning on judging or "fixing" the speaker. For many, silence is the most difficult skill in servant-leader listening. Greenleaf is not only referring to verbal silence but an internal silence that quiets the anxiety of deciding what to say next and allows one's intuition and attentive curiosity to add richness to the silence. Those who knew Greenleaf said that he was comfortable with silence as he continually asked himself the question, "in saying what I have in mind will I really improve on the silence?"

QUESTIONS: Do you respond to any problem by listening first? Why or why not? Are you good at listening to those you want to communicate with? What could you do to listen better?

§§

Language and Imagination

Communicating with others is not as easy as we might wish. Words have their limitations. Alfred North Whitehead once said that "no language can be anything but elliptical, requiring a leap of imagination to understand its meaning in its relevance to immediate experience." It is not enough to say the words. The person who hears the words must make some sort of meaning out of them. The listener must make a leap of imagination and connect the words to his or her own experience. One of the arts of communicating is to say just enough to make that leap possible. Many attempts to communicate fail because the communicator tries to say *too much*.

The physicist and philosopher Percy Bridgman takes another view of it when he says "no linguistic structure is capable of reproducing the full complexity of experience..." When complex experience is forced into a single verbal scheme, people "create a purely verbal world in which they can live a pretty autonomous existence, fortified by the ability of many of their followers to live in the same verbal world." This, of course, is what makes a cult—a group of people who define everything in their own way, and isolate themselves from the mainstream. A leader who becomes trapped in his own closed verbal world can lose touch with experience outside of his closed world, and as a result will no longer be able to lead.

§§

KENT: It is easy for cults to exist within organizations—often among the top leaders. They have similar backgrounds and experiences, values, and reference points. They comfortably reinforce each other. But as a result, they may be out of touch with the rest of the organization, or even the rest of society. That limits their relevance, and hence their effectiveness as leaders.

I once worked in a highly professional organization that was part of a national association. The organization had well-defined programs, job descriptions, training, and career paths. My colleagues were good people doing good work. But because they were experienced and committed to the way the organization did things, it was hard for them to reach outside their well-defined world to discover new needs and new ways of doing things. The leadership gradually lost touch with the changing needs of society and those the organization served. It was sad to see.

DON: Greenleaf read Whitehead on language but he personally studied with Alfred Korzybski, who founded the discipline of General Semantics. Korzybski taught that language was a *map* of reality, not reality itself. In his view, confusing the map for the territory was the root of countless misunderstandings and even wars. A person who believes that his language reflects the whole truth is not likely to listen. Greenleaf took to heart Korzybski's advice to add qualifiers like, "as I see it" or "from where I stand" to keep open those closed verbal worlds. One of Greenleaf's favorite qualifiers was, "from my worm's-eye view."

LINDA: Leaders communicate to clarify, persuade and engage. To understand what will entice the listener to catch her train of thought and to hop on board, the servant-leader must recognize what is meaningful to the individual, and what is relevant to his work. Then the servant-leader can connect with his frame of reference in a manner that is compatible with his world view. If this sounds complicated, think of it simply as *finding the hook*. To the finance officer, the hook is the bottom line; to the clinician, healthy lifestyles; to the human resource manager, a satisfied workforce; to a minister, spiritual values. The servant-leader knows what resonates with each employee, and speaks to that. Far from being manipulative, connecting with each person's interests and ideals shows great respect and humility.

QUESTIONS: Have you ever been trapped in your own closed verbal world, out of touch with those outside your world? If so, what was it like? What did you do about it?

§§

Withdrawal—Finding One's Optimum

Some leaders like pressure and some don't. There are those who like pressure so much that they seek it out, and they perform best when they are totally intense. And then there are those who don't like pressure and do not thrive under it. Because they want to lead, they are willing to endure the pressure that comes with leadership. For both groups, the art of withdrawal is useful. To those who like pressure, it is a change of pace; for those who don't like pressure, it is a way of avoiding exhaustion.

To withdraw and reorient yourself, you need to learn the art of systematic neglect. You need to know how to sort out what is more important from what is less important. And you need to be able to distinguish what is important from what is urgent—and attend to the more important, even when there are penalties for neglecting something that is urgent but actually less important. You can govern your life by the law of the optimum (optimum being that pace and set of choices that give you the best performance over a lifespan). Just remember that there are always emergencies, so the optimum includes having a reserve of energy for coping with emergencies.

Pacing oneself by appropriate withdrawal is one of the best approaches to making optimal use of one's resources. The servant-as-leader must constantly ask himself, how can I use myself to serve best?

You need to learn the art of systematic neglect.

§§

ISABEL: Personal growth will always require time for reflection and withdrawal. In the heat of constant activity which is often controlled by our mind, a powerful instrument, we can miss nuance, beauty, and regeneration. Most of us have struggled with a problem that seemed to have no solution only to awake refreshed with what now seems like an obvious answer that we were unable to see before. Knowing others is knowledge; knowing oneself is wisdom. Activity keeps self-knowledge at bay and relies on the mental and physical aspects of our being. The emotional and spiritual aspects of our being end up getting short shrift. And we are then less than we can be.

If stillness does not capture us, our minds will, and who knows where they will take us. If we take no time to reflect and slow down so we can see clearly, our minds can mislead us. I am often reminded of the Greek philosopher who once said, "our minds have become so polished that there is no longer room for truth to reside there." I think reflection can help us to find truth.

DON: Withdrawing to move ahead seems counter-intuitive. In truth, it is a tool to access intuitive wisdom. Abundant studies document how creative breakthroughs frequently happen while a musician, scientist, or artist is doing something not related to the task at hand, like driving, taking a shower, even sleeping. (The melody for the song "Yesterday" came to Paul McCartney in a dream.) In the early 1970s servant leadership guru Dr. Ann McGee-Cooper taught NASA scientists and astronauts at Purdue to daydream 15 minutes a day, an experiment that was wildly successful in producing concrete results. Withdrawal gives all of us the resources to identify the important so we can control our lives for optimum service.

KENT: I think "the art of systematic neglect" that Greenleaf discusses is a real challenge. We want to do our jobs, and do them well, but there is more to do than we can get done. We cannot survive—we cannot give proper attention to priority issues—unless we neglect lower priority issues. It's hard to do some things poorly, or not at all, even when we believe that they are less important. And yet, we can't do it all, so we have to neglect the things that we can best afford to neglect.

This was hard for me to learn. I learned it as the director of a state government agency. The director's office received about a hundred phone calls per day, sometimes more, and the daily mail could stack as high as one or two feet per day. The solution, of course, was to delegate as much as possible to others in the department. I was fortunate to have two excellent assistants who tracked the calls and the incoming mail and decided who in the department to refer them to for advice or direct response. Even then, I knew that there were problems and opportunities that our department just didn't have the time and resources to handle. We just hoped that the things we *didn't* do were really less important than the things we *did* do.

DUANE: In 1991, Ann McGee-Cooper and I wrote a book, *You Don't Have to Go Home from Work Exhausted!* We had been working with both large and small organizations for years extolling the virtues of servant leadership. In the process, we discovered a truth that Robert Greenleaf suggests in this passage—rest, renewal, and "getting away from it all" is essential for servant-leaders. In our work, we found many leaders in burnout, and they felt it was simply the norm in leading fast-paced, demanding organizations. But Greenleaf asks, "when you are tired, to the point of exhaustion, no matter how noble your intentions are, can you really listen, be empathetic, mentor others, and make good decisions that create a better organization or society?" He wisely tells us to pace ourselves with appropriate withdrawal to renew our energy and spirit, and even more importantly, to have a reserve for coping with emergencies.

While working with organizations, we also learned that servant-leaders are in the highest risk category for burnout. Why? Because they care so much and are passionate about their work. Enthusiasm can override the signals that our bodies give us that we need rest. And too many times, great servant-leaders hit the wall before they see these warning signs. "The servant-as-leader must constantly ask himself, how can I use myself to serve best?" Sometimes the answer is "take a vacation."

LINDA: In too many meetings these days, the group leader finds himself competing with laptops, smartphones, and other devices. Often, it's the leader who encourages (or demands) this behavior. Contemporary work life rewards a pace that is largely unsustainable. Thomas Merton called the pace of the modern world "just another small violence to the spirit." Withdrawal and reflection are where the struggles are brought to peace and the obscurities are brought to light.

The business case for withdrawal argues for wiser decisions and more creative thoughts. Leaders who model withdrawal give their employees permission to disconnect and encourage a healthier workforce.

An important aspect of withdrawing is *disconnecting*. This may entail saying "no" to bosses and colleagues who don't understand the meaning of personal time; who expect us to be perpetually on call. The ability to withdraw is a vital characteristic that allows servant-leaders to refresh, reorient and recharge, if only for a moment.

Finding time for regular withdrawal and reflection is a challenge for executives, who are already working long hours. Carve out the time anyway! Other leaders find the introspection uncomfortable: they would rather be handling a crisis than plumbing their own inner depths. Stretch your comfort zone!

QUESTIONS: Do you work better under pressure, or not? Do you find withdrawal useful to you? Why? Do you have a reserve of energy for coping with emergencies?

§§

Acceptance and Empathy

According to the dictionary, *acceptance* is receiving what is offered with approval, satisfaction, or acquiescence. *Empathy* is the imaginative projection of one's own consciousness into another being. The opposite of both is the word *reject*, to refuse to hear or receive—to throw out.

The servant always accepts and empathizes, never rejects. The servant as leader always empathizes, always accepts the person. However, the servant sometimes refuses to accept some of the person's effort or performance as good enough.

A college president once said that "an educator may be rejected by his students and he must not object to this. But he may never, under any circumstances, regardless of what they do, reject a single student."

We have known this a long time in the family. For a family to be a family, no one can ever be rejected. Robert Frost in his poem "The Death of the Hired Man" states the problem in a conversation on the farmhouse porch between the farmer and his wife about the shiftless hired man, Silas, who has come back to their place to die. The farmer is irritated about this because Silas was lured away from his farm in the middle of the last haying season. The wife says this is the only home he has. They are drawn into a discussion of what a home is. The husband gives his view:

Home is the place where when you have to go there
they have to take you in!

The wife sees it differently. What is a home? She says,

I should have called it something you somehow
haven't to deserve.

Because we all have our weaknesses, the great leader (whether it is the mother in her home or the head of a vast organization) would say what the wife said about home in Robert Frost's poem. It is a mark of true greatness when a leader has a genuine interest in and affection for his followers. It is clearly something the followers "haven't to deserve." Great leaders may have gruff, demanding, uncompromising exteriors. But deep down inside the great ones have empathy and unqualified acceptance of those they lead.

Acceptance of the person, though, requires a tolerance of imperfection. Anybody could lead perfect people—if there were any. But there aren't any perfect people.

It is a part of the puzzle of human nature that the "typical" person is capable of great dedication and heroism *if* he is wisely led. Many people who might otherwise be capable of leading others are disqualified to lead because they cannot work with and through flawed people—which is all there are. The secret of institution building is the ability to bring together a team of imperfect people by lifting them up to grow taller than they would otherwise be.

People grow taller when their leaders empathize with them and accept them for who they are. This is true even

People grow taller when their leaders empathize with them and accept them for who they are.

though their performance may not be as good as it could be. Leaders who empathize and who fully accept those who go with them on their journey are more likely to be trusted.

§§

PAT: When I look out at our country today, it is obvious that our society needs to heal. Acceptance and empathy is the only course of treatment that will restore us and help us thrive. They form the basis of healthy relationships. They demand trust. They insist that we look beyond our differences to find our commonality.

DON: I have never heard someone say, "I trust my boss as a leader because he rejects me as a person." I have, however, heard this comment: "I trust my boss and work my heart out for him because he accepts me, even though he sometimes calls me out when I make mistakes and don't live up to the standards that he holds for both me and himself." What Greenleaf does not say here but does say in other places is that a leader learns to tolerate imperfection after he has identified it in himself through rigorous inner work.

KENT: Greenleaf worked in personnel at AT&T, and did personnel assessment. He knew that people are flawed, imperfect. But he also knew that a servant-leader can connect with people, empathize and accept them, and inspire them to grow taller. People can tell if you believe in them. When you do, it tends to become a positive self-fulfilling prophecy—the people you believe in tend to perform better, giving you even more reasons to believe in them.

CHERYL: When I joined Popeyes, the place needed an attitude adjustment. The problem? The people we were responsible for leading were viewed as "a pain in the neck." The franchise owners were "difficult." The restaurant teams were "poor performers." The guests were "impossible to please." The board members were "challenging." The investors were "not on our side." The first step in turning around your organization's performance? Think positively about the people you lead. Your attitude will determine the altitude of your performance. You can't serve the people well if you don't have aspirations for the team to be wildly successful.

ISABEL: Over the years, I have heard people in organizations say three basic things: (1) we have no guiding vision, (2) we do not communicate, and (3) we do not trust each other.

As I thought about these issues, I wondered how we might get ahead of such problems. Here is the visual model I created to help guide my work in those organizations.

We always need to define and articulate a guiding sense of purpose that allows us to answer the questions of "why are we here?" and "where are we going?" These are large answers, greater than just setting goals. They are the long-term answers to an institution's reason for being. In the diagram, the purpose is the arch of the model.

At the base are the stories of the people and their work. Wendell Berry, in his book, *What Are People For*, said: "When a community loses its memory, its members no longer know one another. How can they know one another if they have forgotten or have never learned one another's stories? If they do not know one another's stories, how can they know whether or not to trust one another? People who do not trust one another do not help one another, and moreover, they fear one another."

You cannot have a floating arch and a floor and no vertical connectors. So to me the connectors are the practice of hospitality by which the stranger is allowed to be who he or she is. The stranger is not expected to be who *we* are. I think this is the heart of empathy. Because we have built a base of trust through the stories, we can embrace those who are not us.

I learned well the lessons of hospitality from my mother. My mother was a graceful cook—beauty and taste interwoven. One Sunday dinner the gravy was lumpy and my sister and I began to tease my mother about it. She asked us to leave the table and to start doing the dishes. To us, that was very strange. We were still eating! We later found that my aunt, who was visiting, had made the gravy. My mother would not have left the gravy off the table, nor would she have mentioned the lumps. The gravy itself did not matter. It was the gift of the gravy and the gathered community that were the important elements. Truly this is the test of hospitality and of empathy: accepting the gift that others are to us.

QUESTIONS: Do you agree that all people are flawed? Why or why not? Whom do you find it difficult to accept or empathize with? Why? How do you feel about your lack of empathy for them?

§§

Know the Unknowable— Beyond Conscious Rationality

The leader needs to have *a sense for the unknowable* and be able to *foresee the unforeseeable*. The leader knows some things and foresees some things which her colleagues or followers do not know or foresee as clearly. This is partly what gives the leader her "lead," what puts her out ahead and qualifies her to show the way.

Many would attribute these qualities of knowing the unknowable and foreseeing the unforeseeable to mystical or supernatural gifts. Others turn to scientific explanations. But whatever the explanation may be, foresight and intuition are crucial, because the leader never has enough information to make a good decision.

You could get more information if you waited longer or worked harder to get it, but the delay and the cost wouldn't be justified. No matter how hard you try or how long you wait, you can rarely get 100% of the information you need. And, if you wait too long, the situation will change, and you will have to start all over, gathering new information. That's the dilemma you face if you are a hesitant decision maker.

The practical reality is that there usually is an information gap between the information you have and the information you need. The art of leadership rests, in part, on the ability to bridge that gap. How do you do that? By intuition. What is intuition? We might say it is the ability

61

to understand something immediately, without the need for conscious reasoning. It is a judgment that comes from an unconscious process. A person who is good at this is likely to emerge as the leader because he or she contributes something of great value. Others will depend on him to go out ahead and show the way because his judgment will be better than most.

Leaders, therefore, must be more creative than most people. Creativity is largely an act of discovery, a push into the uncharted and the unknown. Every once in a while a leader finds herself needing to think like a scientist, an artist, or a poet. And her thought processes may be just as fanciful and as fallible as theirs.

Intuition is a *feel* for patterns, the ability to generalize based on what has happened previously. The wise leader knows when to bet on these intuitive leads, but he always knows that he is betting on percentages—his hunches are not eternal truths.

Intuitive decisions involve anxiety. There is the anxiety that occurs before you make a decision, when you are trying to get as much information as possible. And then there is the anxiety that comes from making the decision itself, knowing that you really didn't have enough information. In addition to the anxiety, there is the pressure that comes from others who want an answer, and want it now.

Trust is at the root of it. Does the leader have a really good information base—both hard data and sensitivity to the feelings and needs of people? Does the leader have a reputation for making consistently good decisions that people respect? Can he de-fuse the anxiety of other people who want more certainty than exists in the situation?

Intuition in a leader is more valued, and therefore more trusted, at the conceptual level. An intuitive answer to an immediate, detailed problem can be a gimmick. Overarching conceptual insight that gives a sounder framework for decisions is the greater gift.

§§

KENT: This is a significant challenge. There is almost always a gap between what we know, and what we would like to know, before we make a decision. The gap can only be covered by intuition. Malcolm Gladwell, in his book, *Blink*, discusses intuition as "how we think without thinking." The best decisions are often those that are impossible to explain to others, because they are intuitive, based on years of experience.

When I think about intuition, I think of the movie *The Man Who Knew Infinity*. It is the story of Indian mathematician Srinivasa Ramanujan, who lived from 1887 to 1920. He was a genius who made extraordinary contributions to mathematics. Entire complex equations would come to him at once. He knew they were right, without having worked out the detailed proofs that explained *why* they were right. Since his death at the age of 32, nearly all of his 3,900 "results" have been proven to be correct. His intuition was incredible.

DON: Greenleaf once taught a class at Dartmouth titled "Intuition in Business Decision Making" that was so popular he was asked to repeat it several times. In that course he stressed the

importance of preparing for an intuitive breakthrough by reading and absorbing all available data, speaking with experts, going
as far as rational analysis will take one, then backing off and
trusting one's *feel* for patterns. There is no shortcut. A leader
who makes a snap decision solely to defuse anxiety is likely not
making the best decision. A servant-leader develops strategies for
knowing the unknowable in order to practice foresight.

ISABEL: The more levels of awareness that one can tap into
allows for a greater sense of intuition. I think this means paying
"radical attention," a favorite phrase of my friend, Rebecca Braden. It's about taking note of all that is happening. I think that
we can train ourselves by using a series of questions:

1. What happened? Make an assessment of the data available. This is a mental and analytical assessment.
2. How does/did it feel? This question asks for an emotional response—a heart answer.
3. What does/did it mean? This question requires a spir-
   itual/purpose answer. It lifts the level of attention to a
   higher level.
4. Now what? This final question is the decision making
   or action question.

Most people with high levels of intuition that results in
good decisions probably go through these questions at the speed
of light. They end up with an intuitive response which in some
ways is grounded in the wholeness of mental, physical, emotional, and spiritual aspects. It is just that there is no need to
discuss it. If you have the grounding, making intuitive decisions
does not mean "shooting from the hip," it means making high
quality decisions.

*A servant-leader develops strategies for
knowing the unknowable.*

QUESTIONS: What does intuition mean to you? When do you rely on your intuition? When do you *not* rely on your intuition? Why?

§§

Foresight—The Central Ethic of Leadership

Foresight is a better than average guess about *what* is going to happen *when* in the future. A leader with foresight has a sort of "moving average" mentality in which past, present, and future are one, bracketed together and moving along as the clock ticks. The process is continuous.

The shape of some future events can be calculated from trend data, but again, there is usually an information gap, so you must cultivate intuition. One is at once, in every moment of time, historian, contemporary analyst, and prophet—not three separate roles. This is what the practicing leader is, every day of his life.

Living this way is partly a matter of *faith*—faith that, if you have the necessary experience and knowledge at the conscious level, then when the situation arises, you will have the intuitive insight that you need. There really isn't any other way, in the turbulent world of affairs (including the typical home), to be calm in the face of uncertainty. Start with the conscious analysis as far as it will take you, and then withdraw, if only for a moment, confident that an insight will come.

Foresight is seen as a wholly rational process, the product of a constantly running internal computer that deals with intersecting series and random inputs and is vastly more complicated than anything technology has yet produced. Foresight means regarding the events of the instant moment and constantly comparing them with a series of projections made in the past and at the same time projecting future events—with diminishing certainty as projected time runs out into the indefinite future.

The failure of a leader to exercise foresight may be viewed as an *ethical* failure. A serious ethical compromise today is sometimes the result of a failure of foresight at an earlier date, when there was freedom to act. The action that society labels "unethical" in the present moment is often one in which there is really no choice. By this standard a lot of guilty people are walking around with an air of innocence, when in fact they were unethical. They failed to foresee events and act constructively when there was still time and the freedom to act.

Foresight is the "lead" that the leader has. Once he loses this lead and events start to force his hand, he is leader in name only. He is not leading; he is just reacting to immediate events, and he probably will not be a leader for long. There are many current examples of the loss of leadership which stems from a failure to foresee what reasonably could have been foreseen, and from failure to act on that knowledge while the leader had freedom to act.

Exercising foresight is not easy. It requires you to live a sort of schizoid life. You have to operate at two levels of consciousness. The first level is involvement in the real world, in which you are concerned, responsible, effective, and value oriented. The second level is detachment from the real world, riding above it, seeing today's events and seeing oneself deeply involved in today's events, but in

*The failure of a leader to exercise foresight
may be viewed as an* ethical *failure.*

the perspective of a long sweep of history and projected into the indefinite future.

Such a split enables one better to foresee the unforeseeable. From one level of consciousness, each of us acts resolutely from moment to moment on a set of assumptions that then govern our lives. Simultaneously, from another level, these assumptions are examined, in action, with the aim of future revision and improvement. Such a view gives us the perspective that makes it possible for us to live and act in the real world with a clearer conscience.

§§

KENT: Foresight is a difficult subject. Of course, we can watch and listen. We can track changes in the natural environment and changes in technology. We can study data on economic, social, political, and demographic trends, including health and disease. We can network with others, and listen to their views of the future. Still, we don't know for sure what will happen. We take action based on the facts and our own intuition.

Foresight is difficult for individual organizations in their customer or service areas, but when we look at world trends, many important futures are not that hard to figure out. We know a lot about world population growth, economic inequality, starvation, and disease. We are learning more about climate change, and the likelihood that a rising sea level will require the relocation of millions of people who live in coastal cities. We know that HIV/AIDS will continue to spread, and we have an idea which continents will be affected next. We know about the rise in obesity, stress, and alienation. We know about cultural and religious differences, and the need for mutual understanding and respect. We don't know enough, but we know a lot. The real question is, what are we doing about it?

I agree with Greenleaf that "the failure of a leader to exercise foresight may be viewed as an *ethical* failure." My experience is that even when leaders have foresight, they may have personal reasons for not acting on it. When I was in government, our agency provided marketing money for an industry group. We argued that some of the money was needed to develop new markets that would benefit future industry growth. The industry leaders spent the money instead on marketing that would get near-term results for their companies, making the leaders look good before they moved on to other jobs in other locations. They didn't care about the longer-term future. That struck me as an ethical failure. They didn't care about what the industry and larger economy would need after they moved on.

DON: Greenleaf was not the first to identify foresight as an *ethical* concern for leaders. The Iroquois Confederacy Constitution, much admired by Ben Franklin, admonished its leaders to "look and listen for the welfare of the whole people and have always in view not only the present but also the coming generations, even those whose faces are yet beneath the surface of the ground—the unborn of the future Nation." Many indigenous people around the globe take a similar extended view of the impact of their decisions, all the way out to seven generations.

ISABEL: It is easy to interpret Greenleaf on foresight and come to the conclusion that he means better planning, more insightful trend analysis and market projections. He is never that simple. He is asking for a higher, deeper, broader look at leadership and its responsibility to be prescient enough to minimize harm.

I often try to create models for myself to understand him more clearly. The first fact is that we have to exercise foresight ourselves—others can't do it for us. To paraphrase Anthony de Mello in the story "Eat your own fruit" in *The Song of the Bird*: "If you don't want someone to chew your food for you, why would you want someone to do your thinking for you?"

The second fact is that the process of exercising foresight may feel less like an exercise in logic and more like an act of creation or imagination. Henry Mintzberg, in his book, *The Rise and Fall of Strategic Planning*, included this quote from Mozart:

> First bits and crumbs of the piece come and gradually join together in my mind; then the soul getting warmed to the work, the thing grows more and more, and I spread it out broader and clearer, and at last it gets almost finished in my head, even when it is a long piece, so that I can see the whole of it at a single glance in my mind, as if it were a beautiful painting or a handsome human being; in which way I do not hear it in my imagination at all as a succession-were. It is a rare feast. All the inventing and making goes on in me as in a beautiful strong dream. But the best of all is the hearing of it all at once.

My practical self says, map it! So—we look at what is happening or trending (the data), we sense (beyond data; some would call this intuition), apply judgment, and end up with foresight. I think of our best judgment as the sum of four quadrants:

ELEMENTS OF JUDGMENT
in relationship to foresight

EXPERIENCE *The known*	**REFLECTION** *The internal*
FAITH *The unknown*	**LISTENING** *The external*

Although still challenging, this helps me to understand how to take the next steps.

QUESTIONS: What do you foresee for your family or organization in the next five years? The next ten years? What changes in the world do you expect, and why? How do you think those changes will affect you?

§§

Awareness and Perception

Essential to all of this is heightened awareness. What do I mean by that? I mean that you must open wide your perception so that you are more aware of sensory data and other signals from the environment. Awareness has its risks, but it makes life more interesting; certainly it strengthens your effectiveness as a leader. When you are aware, you are more alert, more intensely in contact with the immediate situation. You are able to store away more information that can be used in the future to produce intuitive insights when you need them.

William Blake said that "if the doors of perception were cleansed, everything will appear to man as it is, infinite." Those who have gotten their doors of perception open wide enough often enough know that this statement of Blake's is not mere poetic exaggeration. Most of us move about with very narrow perception—sight, sound, smell, tactile—and we miss most of the grandeur that is in the minutest thing, the smallest experience. We also miss leadership opportunities.

There is danger, however. Some people cannot take what they see when the doors of perception are open too wide, and they had better test their tolerance for awareness gradually. A qualification for leadership is that you can tolerate a sustained wide span of awareness so that you can better "see it as it is."

The opening of awareness is value building and value clarifying, and it strengthens you to meet the pressures of life by helping you to build serenity in the face of stress and uncertainty. The cultivation of awareness gives you the basis for detachment, the ability to stand aside and see yourself in perspective in the context of your own experience, amidst the ever present dangers, threats, and alarms. Then you can see your own peculiar assortment of obligations and responsibilities in a way that permits you to sort out the urgent from the important and perhaps deal with the important.

Awareness is *not* a giver of solace—it is just the opposite. It is a disturber and an awakener. Able leaders are usually sharply awake and reasonably disturbed. They are not seekers after solace. They have their own inner serenity.

§§

DON: *Awareness* as Greenleaf defines it is closely related to "mindfulness," a topic that has become popular in business circles. His understanding of awareness, however, goes deeper than heightened perception, right down to its paradoxical impact on one's inner geography. It builds and clarifies values, but also disturbs and awakens; provides confidence in facing the unknown, but only works when one withdraws to seek intuitive insight in the face of the unknown. *Awareness* is a discipline for adults.

PAT: When I first read Greenleaf's words about awareness, I was struck by the fact that he wasn't so much asking us to know ourselves as he was asking us to recognize the impact that we were having on others while being ourselves. Let me share a personal journey. I tend to get really excited about new approaches that promise to deliver superior outcomes. That excitement translates into passionate appeals about why we should adopt the new approaches. I realized a few years back that the way I shared my thoughts about those approaches shut down others. I was so passionate about my ideas that they didn't think I would be open to other ideas, so they didn't offer them. Since it is *not* my intention to shut down others, I need to be conscious of my impact on others and figure out how to invite their ideas. I think that's the kind of awareness Greenleaf is describing.

LARRY: General awareness, and especially self-awareness, strengthens the servant-leader. Making a commitment to foster awareness can be scary—you never know what you may discover. Awareness also aids one in understanding issues involving ethics and values. It lends itself to being able to view most situations from a more integrated, holistic position.

KENT: One of the things I really like about Greenleaf is that he understood the stress and uncertainty experienced by leaders. He understood that there are "dangers, threats, and alarms." If you understand what is going on, you are going to be "reasonably disturbed." But you can still achieve inner serenity. You can learn to stand back, and be more detached, and put it in perspective. You can sort out the urgent from the important. Greenleaf repeatedly sends the message that the world of leadership is a messy, stressful world, but you can still serve. You can still do what servant-leaders do, and do it well.

QUESTIONS: How can you become "more aware of sensory data and other signals from the environment?" If you become more aware, do you agree that you may become "reasonably disturbed"?

§§

A leader must have more confidence in facing the unknown than those who accept her leadership. This is partly anticipation and preparation, but it is also a very firm belief that in the stress of real-life situations, you can still compose yourself in a way that permits the creative process to operate.

This is told dramatically in one of the great stories of the human spirit—the story of Jesus when confronted with the woman taken in adultery. In this story Jesus is seen as a man, like all of us, with extraordinary prophetic insight of the kind we all have some of. He is a leader; he has a goal—to bring more compassion into the lives of people.

In this scene the woman is cast down before him by the mob that is challenging Jesus's leadership. They cry, "the *law* says she shall be stoned, what do *you* say?" Jesus must make a decision, he must give the *right* answer, *right* in the situation, and one that sustains his leadership toward his goal. The situation is deliberately stressed by his challengers. What does he do?

He sits there writing in the sand—a withdrawal device. In the pressure of the moment, having assessed the situation rationally, he assumes the attitude of withdrawal that will allow creative insight to function.

He could have taken another course; he could have regaled the mob with rational arguments about the superiority of compassion over torture. A good logical argument can be made for it. What would the result have been had he taken that course?

He did not choose to do that. He chose instead to withdraw and reduce the stress—during the event itself—in order to open his *awareness* to creative insight. And a great one came, one that has kept the story of the incident alive for two thousand years—"Let him that is without sin among you cast the first stone."

§§

KENT: Many leaders and managers don't take the time to reflect when they are in a challenging situation. People may be pressing them for answers, for action, for a decision. One problem is that in a crisis, one's biochemistry can change—the fight or flight response. When that happens, blood flows to your arm and leg muscles, so you can fight or flee. That makes it harder to think clearly.

I have learned that in most situations, you will have time to reflect, and you *need* to reflect. You need to withdraw and give your biochemistry time to stabilize after the adrenaline rush. Ten minutes makes a difference; an hour is better. Depending on the situation, a day or two, or a week or two, is appropriate. Yes, people inside and outside of your organization may be pushing you to be a "real" leader and make a quick, bold decision. But it could easily be the wrong decision, made too soon, with too little thought. The goal is not a quick decision but a good one, and if possible, a *wise* one. Take your time. Do what Greenleaf said: withdraw and reflect.

DUANE: For centuries, theologians have pondered the meaning of the story of the woman caught in adultery. Themes of forgiveness, judgment, and living a moral life have been the subject of many a sermon. But it is interesting that when Greenleaf offers this story he focuses on Jesus writing in the sand—a withdrawal device to reduce stress, open awareness, and provide creative insight. It was an opportunity, if only for a few seconds, for Jesus to go "inside" and reflect before taking action on the outside.

For years, I focused on the "outer journey" of servant leadership— the tools and skills that would help me work with others in a more serving way. As we work in the leadership development world, there is a strong bias toward taking action. The clock is ticking; we need servant leadership tools that produce action.

I learned that I needed a different focus when Ann McGee-Cooper, my business partner of thirty-eight years, was diagnosed with terminal brain cancer. The thought of losing one of the most important people in my life turned my world upside down. And through the help of some great servant-leader mentors, I realized that what I needed most was to work on the "inner journey" of servant leadership to create a strong grounding that would see me through the loss that was inevitably coming. I didn't have the luxury of taking a sabbatical from work, but Greenleaf's words about this story made an impression: "Jesus chose to withdraw and reduce the stress—*during the event itself*—in order to open awareness to creative insight."

For the next twelve months, I reached out to friends in the servant leadership movement. I read about others' journeys, practiced mindfulness techniques, meditated, prayed, reflected, journaled, and opened my awareness to experience as it unfolded with Ann. But above all, I gained a new respect for the *inner work* that is required of servant-leaders if we are to do the outer work in our organizations. The passage from Greenleaf explains this balance. If we listen, the insights that come from inner reflection can stick around for two thousand years.

LINDA: In this story, Jesus was in a tough spot: he knew he would be judged by the response he made. So he took a moment to contemplate, not only what the right answer would be, but how to give it in a way his detractors could *hear*. He withdrew for an instant—to master his emotions, to sidestep confrontation, to give the accusers space to reconsider.

How often are "bosses" expected to have all the answers? The pressure is on to always know what to do, always have the right words and the brightest ideas, and to have them instantaneously. Servant-leaders withstand the temptation to react precipitously. In humility, they can admit they don't know, ask for help, weigh the options. Those who regularly practice reflection or meditation can more easily access a greater consciousness that will inspire the most insightful solutions. Jesus didn't wait for "analysis paralysis" to set in. A quiet step back provided the needed perspective.

What can't be ignored in this story is the exercise of mercy. Leaders can get fidgety about the concept of mercy. What about justice? Does mercy make me a dupe? Will employees take advantage of me? Will my boss lose respect for me?

Nothing in the servant leadership literature suggests that poor performance or bad behavior should be tolerated. But servant leadership is countercultural. When the work world cuts employees no slack, the servant-leader seeks the benefit of the doubt. While traditional leadership urges swift and strict justice, the servant-leader tempers justice with mercy. When the organization shows contempt, the servant-leader shows compassion. Mercy is strength. And here's another subversive thought: mercy is never earned; it is freely given.

LARRY: Servant leadership can serve as a bridge between people of differing faiths and philosophies. People are able to come together in a shared commitment to serving and leading others. Over the past thirty years I have met servant-leaders who adhered to Christian, Jewish, Muslim, Buddhist, agnostic, secular humanist, and other faith or philosophical traditions. In fact, I believe that as impactful as servant leadership has been as it nears the fifty-year mark, there is still a much greater leap forward to be made. The language of servant leadership can potentially act as a unifying force for people of different faith backgrounds who sometimes seem to be divided by walls.

QUESTIONS: In the stress of real-life situations, are you able to withdraw and reflect? If so, what are the benefits? If not, what are the barriers to withdrawal and reflection?

§§

Persuasion—Sometimes One Person at a Time

Leaders work in wondrous ways. Some quietly deal with others, one person at a time. Such a man was John Woolman, an American Quaker, who lived through the middle years of the eighteenth century. He is known to the world of scholarship for his journal, a literary classic. But in the area of leadership, he is the man who almost singlehandedly rid the Society of Friends (Quakers) of slaves.

It is difficult now to imagine the Quakers as slaveholders, as indeed it is difficult now to imagine anyone being a slaveholder. But many of the eighteenth century Quakers were affluent, conservative slaveholders and John Woolman, as a young man, set his goal to rid his beloved Society of this terrible practice. Thirty of his adult years (he lived to age fifty-two) were largely devoted to this. By 1770, nearly one hundred years before the Civil War, no Quakers held slaves.

His method was unique. He didn't raise a big storm about it or start a protest movement. His method was one of gentle but clear and persistent persuasion.

Although John Woolman was not a strong man physically, he accomplished his mission by journeys up and down the East Coast by foot or horseback visiting slaveholders over a period of many years. The approach was not to censure the slaveholders in a way that drew their animosity. Rather his approach was to raise questions: What does the owning of slaves do to you as a moral person? What kind of an institution are you passing on to your children?

Person by person, inch by inch, by persistently returning and revisiting and pressing his gentle argument over a period of thirty years, the scourge of slavery was eliminated from this Society, the first religious group in America formally to denounce and forbid slavery among its members. One wonders what would have been the result if there had been fifty John Woolmans, or even five, traveling the length and breadth of the Colonies in the eighteenth century *persuading* people one by one with gentle non-judgmental argument that a wrong should be righted by individual voluntary action. Perhaps we would not have had the civil war with its 600,000 casualties and the impoverishment of the South. Perhaps we would not have the continuing social problem that is at fever heat one hundred years later with no end in sight. We know now, in the perspective of history, that just a slight alleviation of the tension in the 1850's might have avoided the war. A few John Woolmans, just a *few*, might have made the difference. Leadership by persuasion has the virtue of change by persuasion rather than coercion. Its advantages are obvious.

John Woolman exerted his leadership in an age that must have looked as dark to him as ours does to us today. We may easily write off his effort as a suggestion for today on the assumption that the Quakers were ethically conditioned for his approach. All people are ethically conditioned to some extent—enough to gamble on.

LARRY: Servant-leaders rely on persuasion, rather than using one's positional authority, in making decisions within an organization. The servant-leader seeks to convince others, rather than coerce compliance. This particular element offers one of the clearest distinctions between the traditional authoritarian model and that of servant leadership. The servant-leader is effective at building consensus within groups. As Greenleaf suggests here, this emphasis on persuasion over coercion has its taproot within the beliefs of The Religious Society of Friends (Quakers), the denomination with which Robert Greenleaf was most closely allied.

DON: Persuasion is the preferred mode for the ethical use of power, standing in stark contrast to manipulation and coercion. Aristotle said we persuade in three ways: *logos* (logic), *pathos* (emotion), and *ethos* (the force of one's character). Of the three, he said *ethos* was the strongest persuader. Persuasion "one person at a time" does not happen by piling up evidence. It happens when the one being persuaded has an intuitive feeling of the rightness of a course of action. Neither does it happen when the persuader "holds a baseball bat behind his back" (as Greenleaf once wrote) with an implied threat of penalizing or even firing someone who does not agree. It happens when the persuader is *present*, listens, engages in dialogue, and is open to positions other than the one being advocated.

ISABEL: Persuasion with ethical underpinnings is admirable. With today's social media and marketing culture, I wonder how we can hold this center. I believe this is right but there are still great harms being done today. Some of today's prophetic voices are calling them out, often at great risk.

KENT: The Woolman story is a beautiful story about steady, quiet, faithful work that eventually had a huge impact. It is a good reminder that significant change can take time, and it can be achieved in small, steady steps. We live in a society in which deferred gratification is not always valued, but it is needed all the same. We also live in a society in which people want clear, measurable results. That is often appropriate, but changing lives may be hard to measure, and the results may be years into the future. I have had teachers who had a big impact on my life, but I did not know it until much later—even decades later. We need more Woolmans in our midst. Change almost always takes time, and that requires persistence and faith.

QUESTIONS: Have you ever engaged in a process of change that involved gentle persuasion and took months or years? What was it like? What did you learn?

§§

One Action at a Time— The Way Some Great Things Get Done

Two things about Thomas Jefferson are of special interest. First, as a young man he had the good fortune to find a mentor, George Wythe, a Williamsburg lawyer whose original house still stands in the restored village. George Wythe was a substantial man of his times, a signer of the Declaration of Independence and a member of the Constitutional Convention. But his chief claim to fame is that he was Thomas Jefferson's mentor. Jefferson studied law in Wythe's office. It was probably the influence of Wythe that moved Jefferson toward his place in history and somewhat away from his natural disposition to settle down at Monticello as an eccentric Virginia scholar (which he remained, partly, despite Wythe's influence). The point of mentioning George Wythe is that old people may have a part to play in helping the potential servant-as-leader to emerge at his optimal best.

Perhaps the most significant aspect of Jefferson, more important in history than the Declaration of Independence or his later term as President, was what he did during the Revolutionary War. With the publication of the Declaration the war was on and Jefferson was famous. He was invited to play important roles in the war, but he turned them all down. *He knew who he was* and he was resolved to be his own man. He chose his own role. He

One Action at a Time—The Way Some Great Things Get Done

went back to Virginia and didn't leave the state for the duration of the war.

Jefferson believed the war would be won by the Colonies, that there would be a new nation, and that that nation would need a new system of law to set it on the course that he had dreamed for it in the Declaration of Independence. So he went back to Monticello, got himself elected to the Virginia legislature, and proceeded to write new statutes embodying the new principles of law for the new nation. He set out, against the determined opposition of his conservative colleagues, to get these enacted into Virginia law.

It was an uphill fight. He would go to Williamsburg and wrestle with his colleagues in the legislature until he was slowed to a halt. Then he would get on his horse and ride back to Monticello to rekindle his spirit and write some more statutes. Armed with these new statutes, he would return to Williamsburg and try again. He wrote 150 statutes in that period and got fifty of them enacted into law, the most notable being separation of church and state. For many years Virginia legislators were digging into the remaining one hundred statutes, ready to consider them as new urgent problems arose.

When the Constitution was drafted some years later Jefferson wasn't even around; he was in France as our Ambassador. But then, he didn't have to be around. He had done his work and made his contribution in the statutes already operating in Virginia. Such are the wondrous ways in which leaders do their work when they know who they are, and are willing to move toward their goal one action at a time, with a lot of frustration along the way.

§§

KENT: In the time of Jefferson, men who had social status or wealth but no military background could be given leadership positions in the Army. Jefferson could have been a wartime leader, perhaps even a military commander. But he knew he had something else to offer. He declined the honor and the glory of a wartime role, went home, and wrote statutes that changed American history.

We face a similar situation every time we are invited to take a position that has power, prestige, and a good salary—but is the wrong position for us, because it does not allow us to use our unique talents and does not call upon our passions. A servant-leader knows what she or he has to offer, and stays focused on offering it.

DON: Jefferson's example teaches us that everything counts, especially when individual acts are aligned with visionary goals. Others may not understand the big picture, but that does not dissuade a warrior of the spirit from trying anyway. Greenleaf followed a similar path by joining AT&T after a college professor spoke of how large institutions had taken over many functions of *caring* that were formerly handled by churches, families, and communities. "If you want to change society," said this professor, "do it from within one of these big institutions." Inspired by that possibility, Greenleaf got a job with the world's largest business organization and patiently set about the impossible task of humanizing it. Like Jefferson, he first had to know who he was, what he was trying to do, and how to strengthen his inner resources to do it.

QUESTIONS: What do you have to offer? Are you in a situation in which you can use your gifts for the good of your organization? If you have a goal, are you willing to move toward that goal one action at a time, with a lot of frustration along the way?

§§

Conceptualizing—The
Prime Leadership Talent

Nikolai Frederik Severin Grundtvig, who lived during the first three-quarters of the nineteenth century, is known as the Father of the Danish Folk High Schools. To understand the significance of the Folk High School you need to know something about the history of Denmark. Since it is a tiny country, not many outside it know this history, and fewer know about the seminal contribution made by Grundtvig. A great church dedicated to his memory in Copenhagen confirms that the Danish are aware of what he did for them.

At the beginning of the nineteenth century, Denmark was a feudal and absolute monarchy. It was predominantly agricultural, with a large peasant population of serfs who were attached to manors. Reforms began early in the century, giving the land to the peasants as individual holdings. Later the first steps were taken toward representative government.

At the beginning of the nineteenth century, however, the Danish peasantry was an underclass, dependent on estate owners and government officials. It was without culture and technical skill, rarely able to rise above the level of bare existence. The agricultural reforms that were implemented did not have the support of the peasants, who did not even understand what they were all about. And yet, within a century, the Danish peasantry was transformed into a well-to-do middle class which, politically and socially, took the lead among the Danish people.

Freedom to own land and to vote was not enough to bring about these changes. A new form of education was designed by Grundtvig to achieve this transformation. Grundtvig was a theologian, poet, and student of history. Although he himself was a scholar, he believed in the active practical life. He conceptualized a school, the Folk High School, as a short intensive residence course for young adults that focused on the history, mythology, and poetry of the Danish people. He addressed himself to the masses rather than to the cultured. The "cultured" at the time thought him to be a confused visionary and contemptuously turned their backs on him. But the peasants heard him, and their natural leaders responded to his call to start the Folk High Schools—with their own resources.

For fifty years of his long life Grundtvig vigorously and passionately advocated these new schools as the means whereby the peasants could raise themselves into *the* Danish national culture. And, stimulated by the Folk High School experience, the peasant youth began to attend agricultural schools and to build cooperatives on the model borrowed from England.

Two events provided the challenge that matured the new peasant movement and brought it into political and social dominance by the end of the century. There was a disastrous war with Prussia in 1864, which resulted in the loss of territory and a crushing blow to national aspirations. And then, a little later, there was the loss of world markets for corn, their major exportable crop, as a result of the agricultural abundance of the New World.

Peasant initiative, growing out of the spiritual dynamic generated by the Folk High Schools, recovered the nation from both of these shocks. They transformed their exportable surplus from corn to "butter and bacon," rebuilt the national spirit, and nourished the Danish tradition in the territory lost to Germany during the long years until it was returned after World War I.

All of this, a truly remarkable social, political, and economic transformation, stemmed from one man's conceptual leadership. Grundtvig himself did not found or operate a Folk High School, although he lectured widely in them. What he gave was his love for the peasants, his clear vision of what they must do for themselves, and his long articulate dedication—some of it through very barren years. He passionately communicated his faith in the worth of these people and their strength to raise themselves—*if only their spirit could be aroused*. It is a great story of the supremacy of the spirit.

§§

LARRY: The ability to look at a problem or an organization from a conceptual perspective means that one must think beyond day-to-day realities. For many, this is a characteristic that requires discipline and practice. The traditional manager-leader is focused on the need to achieve short-term operational goals. Someone who wishes to be a servant-leader must stretch his or her thinking to encompass broader-based conceptual thinking.

ISABEL: In this Danish example, a better society emerged through the development and faith in the people. Spirits were aroused and real change took place. In Greenleaf's writings he envisions a better society, a more just and caring one, and in which the able and less able serve with unlimited liability. That is quite a concept, one that is far above just setting the next goal or achieving the nearest milestone.

I think conceptualization means seeing the whole, its implications, and the way to get there. I can think of many examples of a lack of conceptualization and the negative consequences of this lack—for example, the privatization of prisons, which has turned out to be an immoral act that has little to do with justice and nothing do with mercy. But Greenleaf gives us an affirming, positive example and calls us to do the same. Perhaps it is the rebels in our modern society that see the worth in the people, arouse their spirits, and give them strength to raise themselves. And sometimes—still today—there are risks involved. Greenleaf's examples are of rebels in their time; we just no longer think of them as rebels. We think of them as wise men taking the right actions.

KENT: The most surprising thing about this story, to me, is that Grundtvig never founded or operated a Folk High School. He inspired *others* to do it. The advantage is that when they did it, they had a sense of ownership—the schools belonged to *them*. What does not surprise me is that Grundtvig advocated Folk High Schools for fifty years. It is hard to change the culture of an organization; even harder to change the culture of a nation. It takes long-term commitments like Grundtvig's.

94

DON: Gruntvig's example influenced Greenleaf when he later wrote, "the spirit is power, but only when the spirit carrier, the servant as nurturer of the human spirit, is a powerful and not a casual force." Leaders of organizations often address systemic problems with change strategies, vision statements created by a few folks at a retreat, or new policies proclaimed from the top down (often enforced through penalties rather than inspiration). Seldom do they start with the idea of arousing spirit. Traditional leaders may not believe that the spirit is power and therefore don't trust solutions that can come from the collective wisdom of receptionists and maintenance people, middle managers and machine operators, leaders with and without titles. An ability to *in*-spirit followers helps make a leader a servant-leader.

QUESTIONS: Greenleaf refers to Grundtvig's story as "a great story of the supremacy of the spirit." What does that mean to you? Do you know other stories in which a leader aroused the spirit of a people and helped them to raise themselves?

§§

And Now!

These three examples from previous centuries illustrate very different types of leadership for the common good. They are not suggested as general models for today, although some useful hints may be found in them. What these examples tell us is that the leadership of trail blazers like Woolman, Jefferson, and Grundtvig is so "situational" that it rarely draws on known models. Rather it seems to be a fresh creative response to here-and-now opportunities. Too much concern with how others did it may inhibit us. I don't know what kind of leadership will be seen as seminal one hundred years from now, but I am willing to speculate.

The signs of the times suggest that, to future historians, the coming years will be marked as the period when people of color, the deprived, and the alienated of the world effectively asserted their claims to stature. And that they were led by exceptional people from their own ranks.

It may be that the best that some of today's "privileged" leaders can do is to stand aside and serve by helping when asked *and* as instructed. Even the conceptualizing may be done better, not by an elite as Grundtvig did it in his times, but by leaders from among people of color, the alienated, and the deprived of the world. A possible role for those who are now favored by the old rules may be to make their accumulated wisdom available when people of color and the deprived and the alienated have found their way and freely choose what they find useful from whatever the now-privileged have stored away. Not many of today's privileged may decide to do this. But those who see themselves as *servants first* may want to consider it as the possible best course for them.

I do not know what will come of all this. And I am not predicting a golden age, not soon. But I do believe that *some* of today's privileged who will live into the twenty-first century will find it interesting *if* they can abandon their present notions of how they can best serve their less favored neighbor. They can wait and listen until the less favored find their own enlightenment, then define their needs in their own way and, finally, state clearly how they want to be served. That is how the now-privileged who are natural servants can get a fresh perspective on the priority of other's needs, and thus be able to serve by leading.

For those of today's privileged who feel like joining the fray and serving and leading actively as best they can during what promises to be a long period of unusual turbulence, I suggest that Woolman, Jefferson, and Grundtvig are models to be studied closely. Study them not to copy the details of their methods but as examples of highly creative men, each of whom invented a role that was uniquely appropriate for himself as an individual, that drew heavily on his strengths and demanded little that was unnatural for him, and that was very right for the time and place he happened to be.

§§

DON: An internet search will reveal research that lists "best practices" for educators, nonprofit institutions, health care organizations, and nearly every discipline. Learning best practices of others is a beginning, but rarely a final answer to what one should do in one's local situation. "And now," suggests Greenleaf, "what will be your fresh, creative response to *your* situation? Too much concern with how others did it may inhibit you." Citing best practices is a proven way to give cover for doing the same things. Going out ahead to show the way is a riskier, but nobler alternative.

KENT: Greenleaf is gently dealing with a major issue here. How can the "privileged" help people who are not as "privileged"—in this case, people of color, the deprived, and the alienated? If the privileged want to help, they need to listen to those whom they would help, and take their cues from them. They need to be true servants, assisting others in fulfilling their dreams. Those will not be the dreams of the privileged; those will not be dreams foisted on others by those who feel superior to them.

I have seen this challenge over and over again. The privileged will tend to do what they know how to do, or want to do, rather than what others need them to do. They may have good intentions, but in the end, they are telling others what they should have and what they should do. It may make the privileged feel good, but it shouldn't, because often enough, they aren't helping anyone.

One of my favorite TEDTalks is by Dr. Ernesto Sirolli, titled "Want to help someone? Shut up and listen." Sirolli was a young man working for an Italian non-governmental organization in Zambia back in the early 1970s. He and his colleagues were educated and well-meaning, but they did not stop to listen to the local residents before setting out to teach them how to grow crops in a beautiful valley by the Zambezi River. What happened changed Sirolli's life, and convinced him to become a facilitator of the dreams of others. He decided to do what Greenleaf suggested that the "privileged" should do. He abandoned his previous notions of how he could help his less-favored neighbor, and started listening to people instead. He became a facilitator, serving *their* passions instead of trying to inculcate his own.

PAT: My son was in a fraternity in college that was committed to be of service to the community. One Saturday he and his friends went down to the St. Charles River to bring sandwiches to the homeless. He was down to just chicken salad sandwiches, which he offered to the next person he saw. To my son's surprise, the man wouldn't accept the sandwich. He was still perplexed the next day when he called home. Why wouldn't this man take the sandwich? Perhaps he didn't like chicken salad, I responded. But he's homeless, Mom! Yes, but perhaps his dignity was more important to him than eating something he didn't like.

We are driven to do good, but perhaps the best good is *to serve as asked.*

ISABEL: As I read this passage, I think of people like Rev. William Barber and Moral Mondays, protesting government legislation in North Carolina; Jimmy Carter, who is so often discounted, but has played a role in building homes for the homeless and advancing human rights around the world; the Occupy movement that raised the issue of economic inequality even as the movement was sneered at; the Black Lives Matter movement, which has highlighted the issue of police brutality; and the native tribes gathering around to protest pipelines. There are so many other examples from around the world. Surely the need for servant-leaders is obvious. I also think of the Norse

*We are driven to do good, but perhaps
the best good is to serve as asked.*

word "angr" which means grief or anguish. I sometimes think that if we would listen fully enough to hear the sadness, we could heal many of the ills of our world.

I admire the fact that Greenleaf so clearly calls out the issue of privilege and says that many of the privileged will join in the journey to a more just society. Of course, many will fight against any changes, seeing them as perceived losses to themselves rather than seeing that they can be a better way for everyone. I do not think the power of privilege can be overestimated.

Let me give you a small example. During a teambuilding workshop, we played a game of baseball in which the rules were all the same *except* that anyone could run anywhere anytime the ball was in the air. Teams that primarily consisted of people of color had a good time with these different rules. They are experienced with having the rules changed on them in other situations. The teams that were not people of color were incensed at the rule changes. During the game debrief, we discussed the differences in team reactions. It was a good learning experience.

Anthony deMello in *The Song of the Bird* tells the story of Domesticated Rebels. He ends with this sentence: "A society that domesticates its rebels has gained its peace. But it has lost its future." I think Greenleaf was a rebel in his thinking. The examples he gave in the previous sections were of others who were rebels for the greater good.

LINDA: It may be that the deprived have the greatest chance of success at servant leadership, if they can be convinced that it is not simply another form of subservience. African-American colleagues, for example, who encountered historical deprivation as a population, may have difficulty accepting the label of servant. As one co-worker put it, "I believe in the idea of servant leadership, but I shiver at the terminology." Occupational groups such as nurses, clerks, and secretaries (that these have generally been women is not a coincidence) who have "come up through the ranks," ascended the career ladder step by step, and remember clearly being "under someone's thumb," sometimes worry that servant leadership is a step backward.

There is a difference between *service* and *servitude*. Servitude is coerced; service is a choice. Servitude denies the determination of one's own course; service is a deliberate decision to serve. Choosing service is powerful. Those who have known historical servitude or modest professional beginnings may, owing to their personal struggles, become the best servant-leaders. Given the opportunity, they may draw upon a well of compassion, humility, inclusiveness, and a drive to create the leadership milieu they always sensed was possible.

QUESTIONS: If you are among the "privileged" and you want to serve your less-favored neighbor, what should you do? How do you know? If you are among the "less privileged," how should you serve? How do you know?

§§

Healing and Serving

Twelve ministers and theologians of all faiths and twelve psychiatrists of all faiths convened for a two-day off-the-record seminar on the one-word theme of *healing*. The chairman, a psychiatrist, opened the seminar with this question: "We are all healers, whether we are ministers or doctors. Why are we in this business? What is our motivation?" There followed only ten minutes of intense discussion and they were all agreed, doctors and ministers, Catholics, Jews, and Protestants. "For our own healing," they said.

This is an interesting word, "healing," with its meaning, "to make whole." The example above suggests that one is never really whole. Wholeness is always something being sought. Perhaps, as with the minister and the doctor, the servant-leader might also acknowledge that his own healing is his motivation. There is something subtle that is communicated to one who is being served and led if, implicit in the compact between servant-leader and led, is the understanding that the search for wholeness is something they share.

Alcoholics Anonymous is regarded as a successful path of recovery for more alcoholics than all other approaches combined. Legend has it that the founding meeting to incorporate the organization was held in the office of a noted philanthropist, a very wealthy man. In the course of the discussion of the principles that would guide the new organization, the philanthropist made a statement something like this: "From my experience I think I know about the things that can be done with money and the things that cannot be done with money. What you in A.A. want to do cannot be done with money. You must be poor. You must not use money to do your work."

There was more conversation, but this advice profoundly influenced the course of A.A. The principles that have guided the work of A.A. over the years were born at that meeting: they will be poor; no one but an alcoholic can contribute money to A.A.'s modest budget; and A.A. will own no real property. The essential work of A.A. is that one who is recovered (or partly recovered) will help another toward recovery, and that work will not be done for money.

Here are two quite different perspectives on healing and serving. Whether one is a professional or amateur, the motive for the healing is the same—for one's own healing.

§§

KENT: The happiest people I know are busy loving and helping others. That gives them a lot of meaning and purpose in their lives. It keeps them young, motivated, and energized. Some people seem to think that servant-leaders live stoic, dutiful lives of self-denial. The servant-leaders I know are living *joyful* lives. In serving and healing others, we are healed, we are fulfilled, we are made whole.

DON: I was a college student when I heard Martin Luther King speak a few months after winning the Nobel Peace Prize. I had been aware of the injustice of racism but in my naiveté thought it was a social and moral evil that needed to be addressed for *them*—for people of color. Then I heard Dr. King say this: "White people need universal voting rights, integration, and an end to discrimination as much as Black people. They need to escape the limitations of possibilities imposed by the role of oppressor." I was stunned by what was a new idea to me: every group, every person, needed social justice for their own healing as well as the healing of others so we could all cease to be half-people. Authentic servanthood offers the same benefits. It allows the servant to escape the grandiosity that can come with being a helper who focuses on those who are "less fortunate" and become part of an emergent dynamic that includes us all as fellow healers.

DUANE: Many people who read *The Servant as Leader* remember and quote the iconic passages from the essay, but few mention one important section.

Greenleaf knew that we each have potential for greatness, and our shadows live on the flip side of that greatness. Ann McGee-Cooper put it like this: "Our shadows are our strengths we are wearing wrong-side-out." Greenleaf believed that servant-leaders have a responsibility to go inward and uncover those shadows—and there is not only a responsibility but an "implicit compact between the servant-leader and led" that they share this search for wholeness.

Whether we exercise our need to control, wear others out with our verbosity, become unapproachable with our moodiness, or put others down with a snarky comment gift-wrapped in humor, we have a responsibility to deal with our dysfunctional behaviors. And we don't have to do it alone. We can do this inner work and healing together. We can share our failures, our victories, and our insights while we are on the journey of "making ourselves whole."

Larry: Bob Greenleaf wrote a series of six articles on the theme of "Life With a Purpose," which he had first published separately in 1966 in the A.A. "*Grapevine.*" While Greenleaf himself rarely drank alcohol, his experiences with his mother's alcoholism helped to shape his awareness of the fundamental problems that this caused in family relationships. Decades later, Bob met and became friends with Bill Wilson ("Bill W."), co-founder of Alcoholics Anonymous. Greenleaf was impressed with the work of A.A. and appreciated its decentralized structure as an organization. He also understood the power that A.A.'s approach had brought about in transforming the lives of many individuals. The six "*Grapevine*" articles—published separately in 1966—had never before been collected into a single essay. And so, in 2006, I gathered them together and the Greenleaf Center published them as a new essay by Greenleaf titled "Choosing Life with a Purpose."

> **QUESTIONS:** Do you have the experience of finding your own healing in the healing of others? If so, what was it like? Do you agree that the search for wholeness is something that is shared by the servant-leader and the led?

§§

Community—The Lost Knowledge of These Times

People once lived in communities. In the developing world, many still do. We know that human society can be much better than it is in primitive communities. But if the community itself is lost in the process of development, what will we have then? And will it survive? At the moment there seems to be some question. What is our experience?

We used to care for orphaned children in institutions. We have largely abandoned these institutions on the basis that they are not good for children. Children need the love of a real home—in a family, a community.

Now we realize that penal institutions, other than focusing the retributive vengeance of society and restraining anti-social actions for a period, do very little to rehabilitate. In fact they *de*bilitate and return more difficult offenders to society. What are we to do with these people? It is now suggested that most of them should be kept in homes, in community.

We are now beginning to question the extensive building of hospitals. We need some hospitals for extreme cases. But much of the recent expansion has been done for the convenience of doctors and families, not for the good of patients—or even for the good of families. Only community can give the healing love that is essential for health. Besides, the skyrocketing cost of such extensive hospital care is putting an intolerable burden on health-care systems.

The *school*, on which we pinned so much of our hopes for a better society, has become too much of a social-upgrading mechanism that destroys community. Now we are beginning to question the school as we know it, because it has become a specialized institution, separate from community. And much of the alienation and purposelessness of our times is laid at the door of the *school*.

We are in the process of moving away from institutional care for the mentally challenged and toward small community-like homes. Recent experience suggests that, whereas institutions provide mostly custodial care, the small community can actually lift people up, and help them grow.

Now the care of old people is a special concern, because there are so many more of them and they live so much longer. But the current trend is to put them in retirement homes that segregate the old from the larger community. Already there is the suggestion that these are not the happy places that we hoped they would be. Will retirement homes shortly be abandoned as orphan homes were?

As a generalization, I suggest that any human service that requires love cannot be satisfactorily dispensed by specialized institutions that are separate from community—that take the problem out of sight of the community. Both those being cared for and the community suffer.

Love is an indefinable term, and its manifestations are both subtle and infinite. But it begins, I believe, with one absolute condition: unlimited liability! As soon as one's liability for another is qualified *to any degree*, love is diminished by that much.

Institutions are incorporated to limit the liability of those who serve through them. In the British tradition, corporations are not "Inc." as we know them, but "Ltd."— Limited. Most of the goods and services we now depend on will probably continue to be furnished by such limited liability institutions. But any human service where the person being served should be loved in the process requires community, a face-to-face group in which the liability of each for the other and all for one is *unlimited*, or as close to it as it is possible to get.

Trust and respect are highest in communities in which people are truly committed to each other. Trust, respect, and ethical behavior are difficult for the young to learn and for the old to maintain when there is no community. Living in community can generate an exportable surplus of love which the individual may carry into his many involvements with institutions which are usually not communities: businesses, churches, governments, schools.

The opportunities are tremendous for rediscovering vital lost knowledge about how to live in community, while retaining as much as we can of the value in our present urban, institution-bound society. All that is needed to rebuild community is for enough servant-leaders to show the way, not by mass movements, but by each servant-leader demonstrating his own unlimited liability for a quite specific community-related group.

§§

DON: Some lawyers in servant leadership workshops have told me that the phrase "unlimited liability" strikes fear in their hearts. Greenleaf, of course, is not speaking of a legal principle but a principle of love that emerges from community. That prospect can strike fear in the hearts of everyone! To be known is to be vulnerable; to know others is to be in relationships that may call one to action on the others' behalf. In E.B. White's book *Charlotte's Web*, Wilbur the pig asked Charlotte, "why did you do all this for me? I don't deserve it. I've never done anything for you." Charlotte replied, "you have been my friend. That in itself is a tremendous thing."

KENT: My wife and I have travelled in countries in Asia and Africa that are certainly poor by modern standards. People live in small huts, with no electricity or running water. They have few clothes, no TVs or iPads, no refrigerators, no cars or motorcycles, little food, and little access to healthcare. In short, they don't have much. And yet, they have their faith, and they have each other—their families and local communities. Some of them seem remarkably happy. They remind me that, in many ways, what we need, what we *really* need, is each other. We need to love and be loved, and we need to belong.

In the countries we visited, communities are geographic— they are made up of people who live in the same place. Today, in the United States, communities are often relational instead of geographic. One's community may be at a place of worship, or a

110

social club, a professional association, a group that supports an athletic team, people who share a hobby, or one's colleagues at the office. But whatever makes up the community, the fellowship, the loving and caring, are essential to personal growth and healing. As servant-leaders, we can build these communities, whether they are geographic or relational or both.

ISABEL: This section of Greenleaf's essay could have been written today! He names institution after institution that is failing in the dispensation of love, caring, and making lives better. The penal system, particularly the privatized one, has become what Michelle Alexander calls *The New Jim Crow*, which is the title of her book. Charter schools fail to live up to their promise and are complicit in the destruction of community; for-profit universities do not serve the students but encumber them with debt; health care is profit-making rather than healing; and today's churches, which of all places could lead the way, are often major failures. Oh my goodness, it would be easy to give up and see Greenleaf's vision as impossible, following in the steps of Don Quixote, tilting at windmills!

And yet we hear stories that prove to us that "love makes all things possible." I remember the story of the Ku Klux Klan leader who was harassing a Jewish rabbi with the intent of driving him out of town. This story appeared in *The New York Times* in January 2009. Packages arrived at the rabbi's house, full of anti-black, anti-Semitic pamphlets and an unsigned card that read, "The KKK is watching you, scum."

The rabbi responded with love. He learned that the Klansman lived alone, was nearly blind, and used a wheelchair to get around; both of his legs had been amputated because of diabetes. The rabbi called him and called him until finally the Klansman responded. The rabbi and his wife went to see him. The three of them talked for hours, and began to build a relationship. The end—or maybe the beginning—of this story is that the rabbi and his wife eventually invited the Klansman to move into their home, where they cared for him as his health declined. The power of love helped the Klansman to renounce the Klan, give up his hatred of the Jewish people, and convert to Judaism.

And so I know that Greenleaf is right. Not in an abstract sense but in a real practical sense. The power of love, of unlimited liability, one person at a time toward one person, is the key to rebuilding community and communities. We can serve without loving but the qualitative difference is immeasurable when we serve with love as the basis. How can we possibly lose?

In the early 1980s I attended a business conference in New York City on productivity. The keynote speakers were the CEOs of the 100 Best Companies to Work For at that time. I well remember this rather nondescript man with handmade transparencies say: "The reason we are on this list is that we love the people we work with. We love our employees, our partners, our suppliers and everyone we work with. That is why we are on this list." It was the first time I had ever heard anyone use the word "love" and use it authentically in a business conference with a business objective. I remember it still.

Greenleaf captured this thought in the 1970s when he wrote about it. Having studied him, I am sure he thought of it before then. Today we still struggle to put this practice into place. But we must! Perhaps love—unlimited in its liability—is all that will save us.

LARRY: M. Scott Peck, who wrote about the importance of building true community, says the following in *A World Waiting to Be Born:* "In his work on servant-leadership, Greenleaf posited that the world will be saved if it can develop just three truly well-managed, large institutions—one in the private sector, one in the public sector, and one in the nonprofit sector. He believed—and I know—that such excellence in management will be achieved through an organizational culture of civility routinely utilizing the mode of community." From my conversations with Peck, it was clear that he found considerable inspiration in Greenleaf's writings on building community. So do I.

QUESTIONS: What does "community" mean to you? Is it geographic, or relational, or both? What communities mean the most to you? Why?

§§

Institutions

Our task is to rediscover the knowledge of community while we refine and improve the institutional structure that we need to survive. The first order of business is to build a group of people who, under the influence of the institution, grow taller and become healthier, stronger, and more autonomous.

Some institutions achieve distinction for a short time by the intelligent use of people. But it is not a happy achievement, because people are being exploited. That kind of distinction does not last long. Others aspire to distinction by embracing "gimmicks" like profit sharing, work enlargement, information, participation, suggestion plans, paternalism, and motivational management. These are not gimmicks in institutions that build people, but in institutions that use people, they are like aspirin—sometimes stimulating and pain relieving, and with immediate measurable improvements of sorts. But these are not the means whereby an institution moves from people-using to people-building. In fact, an overdose of these "medicines" may seal an institution's fate as a people-user for a very long time.

An institution starts on a course toward people-building with leadership that puts *people first*. With that, the right actions fall naturally into place. And none of the conventional gimmicks may ever be needed.

DON: Greenleaf published the essay *The Institution as Servant* two years after *The Servant as Leader.* The idea that an institution could be a servant, a role identified with individual persons, disturbed many of his business friends. Ironically, he identifies some of the strategies often touted as people-building as mere gimmicks. Apparently the maxim to "put people first" is more radical than it first seems. Ralph C. Stayer, President of Johnsonville Sausage, once said: "Most companies use their people to build the business. We use our business to build our people." No gimmicks there.

KENT: Greenleaf's best test for servant-leaders is whether or not people are growing. He thought that growing people is the fundamental business of any organization. In a paper on "Ethics and Manipulation" that Greenleaf presented at a conference in Switzerland in 1970, he proposed a new business ethic, which was that "the work exists for the person as much as the person exists for the work. Put another way, the business exists as much to provide meaningful work to the person as it exists to provide a product or service to the customer." Greenleaf went on to say that "when the business manager who is fully committed to this ethic is asked, 'What are you in business for?' the answer may be: '*I am in the business of growing people*—people who are stronger, healthier, more autonomous, more self-reliant, more competent. Incidentally, we also make and sell at a profit things that people want to buy so we can pay for all this." When servant-leaders help their colleagues grow and perform at their highest levels, gimmicks aren't needed.

ISABEL: Again, Greenleaf at his gently demanding self! Not good enough to pretend or to act like you care by putting in "caring" programs. He asks that you really care. It is true that people can sometimes be fooled in the short term. Over the long term, it is impossible; we just create cynics who put their best elsewhere. Caring actions only matter if they are real and authentic over time. The answer to the question of the institutional "why" must always be larger than self-serving, if one wants it to withstand the test of time.

LARRY: Greenleaf's ideas are helpful guideposts for understanding what it means to bring servant leadership into an institution and to try to live that out faithfully. One aspect of his essay, *The Institution as Servant*, that has increasingly brought me into conversation with others has been the idea of *primus inter pares*, or "the first among equals." His thinking on the first among equals idea is powerful. He looks at the typical hierarchical model—the "Moses model," as he terms it—and talks about the problems with that approach. Indeed, over the last forty years there has been a general trend to flatten organizations, which has moved us more in the direction of teams and councils.

> **QUESTIONS:** What does it mean to you to "put people first?" What are some specific things you could do so that the people in your organization "grow taller and become healthier, stronger, and more autonomous?"

§§

Trustees

Institutions need two kinds of leaders: those who are inside and carry the active day-to-day roles, and those who stand outside and oversee the active leaders—the *trustees*.

The trustee is what the title implies, a person in whom ultimate trust is placed. Because institutions inevitably include conflict, the trustee is the court of last resort if an issue arises that cannot be resolved by the staff. If physical assets are involved, the trustee is ultimately responsible for their good use. He has a prime concern for the organization's goals and for progress toward those goals.

The trustee makes her influence felt more by knowing and asking questions than by authority, although she usually has authority and can use it if need be. If, as is usual, there are several trustees, their chairperson has a special obligation to see that the trustees as a group sustain a common purpose and are influential in helping the institution maintain a high level of performance toward its goals. The chairperson is not simply the presider over meetings, he must serve and lead the trustees as a group and act as their major contact with the active inside leadership. Although trustees usually leave the "making of news" to active persons in the organization, trustees have an important leadership opportunity.

No one step will more quickly raise the quality of the total society than the reconstruction of boards into groups of able, dedicated servant-leaders. Here are two disturbing questions: If enough able, dedicated servant-leaders become available, will this change actually take place? And are enough able people now preparing themselves for these roles so that this change *can* be made in the event that it is possible to make it?

§§

KENT: I imagine that if Greenleaf were alive today and we met for the first time, he would introduce himself, and then say: "Let's talk about boards." Greenleaf mentioned boards in this first essay; said more about boards in his second essay, *The Institution as Servant;* and then wrote a third essay, *Trustees as Servants*, that was entirely about boards. Why this focus on boards? Greenleaf concluded that boards can be leverage points for positive change. Boards of both private and non-profit corporations have all the legal authority of an organization. They can set policy, lead the corporate planning effort, and choose the administrative leaders. If the members of the board are servant-leaders, the organization can become a servant-institution, and servant institutions can change our world for the better.

ISABEL: Often boards are kept in the dark, and accept this situation willingly in return for the stroking of their own egos by the organization. This does not serve the organization well in the ways that Greenleaf points to: institutions that enlarge and liberate and in the end create a better society. I admire those organizations whose trustees actually make the world a better place and refuse to be mired down in the overwhelming reports that are designed to keep them docile.

In the Southwest, I worked with an organization that built housing for migrant workers. This was their passion and vision. As is obvious, this was not a money maker, so they also built moderate-income housing. When they needed new trustees for their board, the first question was whether or not the person believed in the mission. Without this assurance, a board could have easily decided to do only moderate-income housing. The trustees guarded against this diligently. I think that more organizations should have that kind of clarity. If the vision is purely profit, any path—legal or illegal, ethical or unethical—will get you there. That is not the Greenleaf vision. I believe that is also why his words continue to be so powerful.

LARRY: Servant-led organizations are called to seek a delicate balance between conceptual thinking and a day-to-day, focused approach. Unfortunately, boards can sometimes become involved in the day-today operations and fail to provide the conceptual vision for an institution. Trustees need to be mostly conceptual in their orientation, staffs need to be mostly operational in their perspective, and the most effective CEOs should cultivate both perspectives.

QUESTIONS: Have you ever served on a board? If so, what was it like? How does Greenleaf say that a trustee makes her influence felt?

§§

Power and Authority—The Strength and the Weakness

In a society likes ours, with complex institutions, there are large and small concentrations of power. Sometimes it is a servant's power of persuasion and example. Sometimes it is coercive power used to dominate and manipulate people. The difference is that servant-leaders use power to create opportunities and alternatives for others, so that individuals can make choices and be more autonomous. Power-oriented leaders coerce people into a predetermined path. Even if it is "good" for people, their autonomy is diminished.

Some coercive power is open and brutal; some is hidden and subtly manipulative. Most of us are more coerced than we know. We need to acknowledge that, in an imperfect world, authority backed up by power is necessary because we just don't know a better way. We may one day find one. It is worth searching for.

The trouble with coercive power is that it only strengthens resistance. And, if successful, its controlling effect lasts only as long as the force is strong. It is not organic. Only persuasion and the consequent voluntary acceptance are organic.

Since both kinds of power have been around for a long time, an individual will be better off if at some point he is close enough to raw coercion to know what it is. One must be close to both the bitterness and goodness of life to be fully human.

One must be close to both the bitterness and
goodness of life to be fully human.

The servant, by definition, is fully human. The servant-leader is functionally superior because he is closer to the ground—he hears things, sees things, knows things, and his intuitive insight is exceptional. Because of this he is dependable and trusted. And he knows the meaning of that line from Shakespeare's sonnet: "They that have power to hurt and will do none...."

§§

ISABEL: In workshops when I have asked people to describe their best or worst boss, there are significant distinctions, and they relate to the use of power by that person. The best boss listens, shares, helps, and makes the person better. The worst boss can best be described as a "petty tyrant" or one who uses coercive power and manages by fear and intimidation. This person is often described as manipulative and negative.

In the Carlos Castaneda books, he says that when we are in the presence of petty tyrants, we must be very careful, for they have the power to destroy the fragile being. We also learn awareness from them, and at the very least we learn that we do not want to be like them. Greenleaf points us in this same direction, and lays out the way to be better—to serve with unconditional liability.

KENT: Servant-leaders do not seek power, they seek to make a difference in the lives of others. That's why Greenleaf referred to the servant's power of persuasion and example. He said that "servant-leaders use power to create opportunities and alternatives for others, so that individuals can make choices and be more autonomous." For servant-leaders, then, power is only a means, not an end; only a tool, not a goal. And when servant-leaders exercise power, they do not exercise it for their own personal benefit, they exercise it on behalf of others. They engage in a process of discussion, persuasion, and consensus-building that allows them to exercise power *with* people, not *over* people.

QUESTIONS: What are the problems with coercive power? What are the benefits of persuasion? What kind of power do you use most often? How has that worked for you? How has it worked for the people around you?

§§

How Does One Know the Servant?

Who is the servant? How does one tell a truly giving, enriching servant from the neutral person or the one whose net influence is to diminish other people?

A distinguished rabbi and scholar had just concluded a lecture on the Old Testament prophets in which he had spoken of true prophets and false prophets. A questioner asked him how one tells the difference between the true and the false prophets. The rabbi's answer was succinct and to the point. "There is no way!" he said. Then he elaborated. "If there were a way, if one had a gauge to slip over the head of the prophet and establish without question that he is or he isn't a true prophet, there would be no human dilemma and life would have no meaning."

So it is with the servant issue. If there were a dependable way that would tell us, "this man enriches by his presence, he is neutral, or he takes away," life would be without challenge. Yet it is terribly important that we *know*, both about ourselves and about others, whether the net effect of our influence on others enriches, is neutral, or diminishes and depletes.

Since there is no certain way to know this, one must turn to the artist for illumination. Such an illumination is in Herman Hesse's idealized portrayal of the servant Leo whose servanthood comes through in his leadership. In stark modern terms it can also be found in the brutal reality of the mental hospital in Ken Kesey's novel, *One*

Flew Over the Cuckoo's Nest. Kesey describes Big Nurse— strong, able, dedicated, dominating, authority-ridden, manipulative, exploitative. The net effect of her influence is to diminish other people, literally destroying them.

In the story she is pitted in a contest with tough, gutter-bred MacMurphy, a patient at the hospital. MacMurphy has a way of building up people and making both patients and the doctor in charge of the ward grow larger as persons, stronger, healthier—an effort that ultimately costs MacMurphy his life. If one will study the two characters, Leo and MacMurphy, one will get a measure of the range of possibilities in the role of servant as leader.

§§

LINDA: Let's stay with the *Cuckoo's Nest* story for a moment. I have long been fascinated by Big Nurse, or Nurse Ratched, perhaps because my original education was as a nurse. If you haven't watched the film recently, do it, or in the interest of time, visit the "Therapy Scene" on YouTube. Then ask yourself these questions:

- If you were a participant in the therapy group, how would you feel about the experience? How would you feel about Nurse Ratched?
- Who was the real leader in the group?
- Understanding that there are boundaries to maintain, could Nurse Ratched have handled the situation differently?

- What is Nurse Ratched's philosophy of power versus service?
- Do you think she went into nursing with this philosophy, or did it evolve? How does that happen?
- And what about the associate nurse? Why did she remain in the background? Could she have been a constructive influence?

How do we know the servant? The Bible says, "by their fruits you shall know them." The nurse in the position of authority, in a vocation of caring, is not what she seems, as we can tell by her actions. The patient, with an unsavory history and in a position of complete dependence is not what he seems, as we can tell by his actions. Our expectations are reversed. Servant-leaders can come from the strangest places!

How would the people we lead answer those questions about us? Are we in danger of becoming Nurse Ratched? The highest of ideals, the best of intentions, can be corroded by the disappointments and failures of the world and the workplace. The ensuing hopelessness, cynicism or misuse of authority can kill the spirit of service. Servant-leaders have a moral duty to guard their spirits and to nurture them.

How do we know if we are servant-leaders? Only when the people we lead see us that way.

DON: You can identify the skills and capacities of a leader who may be a servant: Does the person listen deeply, use persuasion as the preferred mode of power, display conceptual thinking, participate in—and build—community? You can ask what effect this person has on those around her. And you can rely on informed intuition.

ISABEL: How does one know the servant? The effect and affect on others is the test. Are people better or worse because we are there?

KENT: When I am speaking in public, I am often asked if specific national leaders are servant-leaders. I can't answer. TV sound bites, news broadcasts, editorials, and ads are simply not a substitute for getting to know someone personally on a daily basis. Fortunately, I have had the privilege of getting to know many servant-leaders by working with them day after day. Before long, it became pretty clear why and how they made their decisions, and how they treated people. I could tell that they had the desire to serve, and were doing their best to have a positive impact on others.

QUESTIONS: Are there servant-leaders in your own life? How can you tell? How soon after meeting them did you know that they were servant-leaders?

§§

In Here, Not Out There

A king once asked Confucius for advice on what to do about the large number of thieves. Confucius answered, "If you, sir, were not covetous, although you should reward them to do it, they would not steal." This advice places an enormous burden on those who are favored by the rules, and it establishes how old is the notion that the servant views any problem in the world as *in here*, inside himself, not *out there*. If a flaw in the world is to be remedied, the servant knows that the process of change starts *in here*, in the servant, not *out there*.

So it is with joy. Joy is inward; it is generated inside. It is not found outside and brought in. It is for those who accept the world as it is—part good, part bad—and who identify with the good by adding a little island of serenity to it.

Herman Hesse dramatized it in the powerful leadership exerted by Leo. He appeared to only serve in menial ways, but by the quality of his inner life that was manifest in his presence, he lifted people up and made the journey possible for them. Camus, in his final testament quoted earlier, leaves us with "each and every man, on the foundations of his own sufferings and joys, builds for them all."

§§

DON: Whoever you are, you can be an authentic servant-leader by learning necessary disciplines, beginning with listening, the "premier skill of a servant-leader." Greenleaf gave us an ideal, not a prescription, and was fully aware he was not a servant-leader all the time in all situations, although he improved with experience.

LINDA: Servant leadership, while indisputably material and practical, also reflects elements of the metaphysical. The characteristics of humility, reflection and introspection, intuition and foresight are a few examples. Servant-leaders cultivate an interior life that supports and sustains their exterior life.

As servant-leaders, we must accept the awesome reality that our actions shape the world around us. If we believe something is true, we must act accordingly. If we understand that all thoughts create form on some level, we must think differently. If we recognize the repercussions of our words, we must speak more carefully. If we wish to create a unified environment, we must behave in ways that are unifying. If we comprehend that our decisions affect a myriad of others, we must lead in ways that uplift our workplace. *We cannot profess a truth and fail to be changed by it.*

The rewards of servant leadership are both extrinsic and intrinsic, in the celebration of creating new leaders and in the quiet joy of service itself.

KENT: It is hard to read the first paragraph of this section without thinking of the quote attributed to Gandhi: "Be the change that you wish to see in the world." The change starts *in here.* And the person who starts the change doesn't have to be the president or CEO of an organization. The simple fact is that anyone can be a servant-leader, because anyone can identify and meet the needs of others. Anyone can start the change process.

PAT: We must avoid the temptation to blame. There is nothing productive in blame. It creates distance between people and solves nothing.

ISABEL: So we come back to the fact that it all begins with us. None of us are saints, but we can become better by truly listening to others, and allowing for that transformation to take place. As long as we defend only our own long-held beliefs, there will be no justice, no peace and certainly no joy. Surely the better way is the way of the servant, with a lightness of spirit. Surely the better way is the journey to wholeness that embraces the good in us and in others.

QUESTION: What does it mean to you when Greenleaf says that "the servant views any problem in the world as *in here*, inside himself, not *out there*?"

---

§§

Who is the Enemy?

Who is the enemy? Who is holding back our progress toward the better society that is reasonable and possible using available resources? Who is responsible for the mediocre performance of so many of our institutions? Who is standing in the way of a larger consensus on the definition of the better society and paths to reaching it?

Not evil people. Not stupid people. Not apathetic people. Not the "system." Not the protesters, the disrupters, the revolutionaries, the reactionaries.

I grant that fewer evil, stupid, or apathetic people or a better "system" might make the job easier. But their removal would not change matters, not for long. The better society will come, if it comes, with plenty of evil, stupid, apathetic people around and with an imperfect, ponderous, inertial-charged "system" as the vehicle for change. Liquidate the offending people, radically alter or destroy the system, and in less than a generation they will all be back.

A society cannot be "cleaned up" once and for all according to an ideal plan. And even if it were possible, who would want to live in a sterile world? Evil, stupidity, apathy, the "system" are not the enemy even though society-building forces will be contending with them all the time. The healthy society, like the healthy body, is not the one that has taken the most medicine. It is the one in which the internal health building forces are in the best shape.

The real enemy is fuzzy thinking on the part of good, intelligent, vital people; their failure to lead; and their failure to follow servants as leaders. Too many settle for being critics and experts. There is too much intellectual wheel spinning, too much retreating into "research," too little preparation for and willingness to undertake the hard and high-risk tasks of building better institutions in an imperfect world. There aren't enough people who understand that "the problem" is *in here* and not *out there*.

In short, the enemy is strong natural servants who have the potential to lead but do not lead, or who choose to follow a non-servant. They suffer. Society suffers. And so it may be in the future.

§§

KENT: This is where the rubber hits the road. We act, or we don't. We sit back, or we sit up. Greenleaf challenges us to stop talking about it and start doing it. As Edmund Burke said, "all that is necessary for the triumph of evil is that good men do nothing." The enemy is those who could be servant-leaders, but do not serve.

We don't have time to fight every fight. For that matter, not every fight is worth fighting. We need to pick the fights that we think are most important and contribute whatever time, resources, and skills we can contribute. We may not know how it will come out. We may not win the fight. But we can be authentic, and take a stand based on our values and our desire to make life better for others.

DON: This is not a traditional self-help, motivational passage. Yes, it is a call to action, but also a call to *depth*. Rebecca Braden, who has taught servant leadership around the globe for more than twenty years, tells me, "I began sorting servant leadership into three 'buckets' or 'landscapes'—the Internal Landscape, the External Landscape, and the Future Landscape. I believe the quality of the servant's actions and *behaviors* in the second and third, emanate from the first. No surprise there, right? So I try to be disciplined in maintaining that landscape first and foremost."

> **QUESTION:** Greenleaf asks: "Who is the enemy?" Do you agree with his answer? Why or why not?

§§

Implications

The future society may be just as mediocre as this one. It may be worse. And no amount of restructuring or changing the system or tearing it down will change this. There may be a better system than the one we now know. It is hard to know. But, whatever it is, if we do not have the people who can lead it well, a better system will not produce a better society.

It is simple: *able servants with potential to lead must lead and, where appropriate, they must follow only servant-leaders.* Not much else counts if this does not happen.

Realistically, there must be some order. The great majority of people will choose some kind of order over chaos, even if it is delivered by a brutal dictator and even if, in the process, they lose much of their freedom. Therefore the servant-leader must pursue a path that includes order. The big question is, what kind of order? This is the great challenge to the emerging generation of leaders: Can they build better order?

An older person who grew up in a period when values were more settled and the future seemed more secure will be disturbed by much he finds today. But one firm note of hope comes through, loud and clear. We are at a turning point in history in which people are growing up faster. Some extraordinarily able, mature, servant-disposed men and women are emerging in their early and middle twenties. The percentage may be small, or it may be larger than we think. And it is not an elite; it is all sorts of exceptional people. Most of them could be ready for some large society-shaping responsibility by the time they are thirty *if* they are encouraged to prepare for leadership as soon as their potential as builders is identified.

Preparation to lead does not need to be at the complete expense of vocational or scholarly preparation, but it must be the *first priority*. And it may take some reallocation of resources and a lot of initiative on the part of these people to accomplish all that should be accomplished *and* give leadership preparation first priority. But whatever it takes, it must be done. For a while at least, until a better led society is assured, some other important goals should take a subordinate place.

All of this rests on the assumption that the only way to change a society is to produce people, enough people, who will change it. The urgent problems of our day are here because of human failures—individual failures, one person at a time failures.

The new "system" will be whatever works best. The builders will find the useful pieces wherever they are, and invent new ones when needed. This will be done without reference to ideology. "How do we get the right things done?" will be the question of the day, every day. And all men and women who are touched by the effort will grow taller, and become healthier, stronger, more autonomous, *and* more disposed to serve.

Leo, the servant and the exemplar of the servant-leader, has one further portent for us. If we assume that Herman Hesse is the narrator in *Journey to the East*, at the end of the story he establishes his identity. His final

The only way to change a society is to produce people, enough people, who will change it.

confrontation at the close of his initiation into the Order is with a small transparent sculpture, two figures joined together. One is Leo, the other is the narrator. The narrator notes that a movement of substance is taking place within the transparent sculpture:

> ...I perceived that my image was in the process of adding to and flowing into Leo's, nourishing and strengthening it. It seemed that, in time... only one would remain: Leo. He must grow, I must disappear.
>
> As I stood there and looked and tried to understand what I saw, I recalled a short conversation that I had once had with Leo during the festive days at Bremgarten. We had talked about the creations of poetry being more vivid and real than the poets themselves.

What Hesse may be telling us here is that Leo is the symbolic personification of Hesse's aspiration to serve through his literary creations, creations that are greater than Hesse himself. His work, for which he was but the channel, will carry on and serve and lead in a way that he, a twisted and tormented man, could not—except as he created.

Does not Hesse dramatize, in extreme form, the dilemma of us all? Except as we venture to create, we cannot project ourselves beyond ourselves to serve and lead.

To which Camus would add, *create dangerously*!

§§

KENT: Preparing people to lead is a very high priority, as Greenleaf pointed out. Educational institutions commonly claim to be preparing leaders for the future, but often, they do not give them leadership *experience*. When you teach people about baseball, you don't just teach them the rules and the history, and let them watch a game. You get them down on the field to hit and catch balls. Students need experience in identifying and meeting the needs of others. That's what they do in Greenleaf's fable, *Teacher as Servant.* The students who live in Jefferson House have to figure out what people need, and organize other students and the appropriate resources to meet the need. In the process, they gain real leadership experience.

LINDA: The idea that servant-leaders are *not an elite* has special appeal. In order to produce enough servant-leaders to change society and our organizations, the net must be cast widely, and all sorts of people must be invited to lead. Servant leadership has never required one to hold a formal leadership position. In fact, everyone in the workplace should be encouraged to be a servant-leader. We need servant-leaders in communities and families as well. I have come to appreciate that anyone who serves and who goes out ahead to show the way in that service is a servant-leader.

"We are all leaders, all the time," is an aspirational statement, but one that bears consideration. None of us gets a pass. The world cannot afford to allow any of us to watch from the wings. While we may not all be leaders in the classical sense, it's time for everyone to claim their small niche for service; to stand up and show the way. Small service is not trivial service, and those who might resist the large notion of SERVANT LEADERSHIP may be drawn to and accept the modest notion of servant leadership. They are all indispensable. Anyone, in any walk of life, can model a quality of service that inspires others to serve.

In truth, we are often simultaneously leaders and followers. No matter how high we sit in the hierarchy, someone is above us. Servant-leaders discern the symbiotic nature of leading and following. They respect that responsible followership is inherent in the act of leadership.

Preparation as a first priority in the work world is a challenging premise. The urgency of the day prompts us to throw employees into the fray quickly, with less than adequate preparation for their jobs. To prepare them also to serve and to lead, in whatever their capacity, is too seldom on the agenda of managers.

To servant-leaders, the essence of this preparation is foundational. Teaching these tenets to *the many*, even if only *the few* rise to positions of prominence, is a challenge worth undertaking; a creditable return on investment.

On the journey of servant leadership, everyone must be prepared to lead and serve. Everyone must be expected to lead and serve. If society and our organizations have any hope for real change, no one can be left on the side of the road.

DON: At age forty, Robert Greenleaf decided he needed to prepare for his older years *even though he did not know what he was preparing for*. He took every opportunity to learn, meet famous and not-so-famous transformative people, expose himself to the latest artistic movements (with the help of his brilliant wife Esther), read widely, and think deeply. He lived a life of preparation for a role that he trusted would eventually emerge. He lived the principle of creating dangerously, and tried to follow his advice that able servants should "follow only servant-leaders." His writings are not academic but based on the empirical wisdom of his own life. He has moral authority to write what he writes.

QUESTIONS: Greenleaf said that *"able servants with potential to lead must lead and, where appropriate, they must follow only servant-leaders.* Not much else counts if this does not happen." Do you agree? Why or why not?

§§

ISABEL: Looking back on the entire essay, all I can says is: dog-gone Greenleaf! He is so engaging and so right. I am captured before I realize how demanding he really is. Once you truly engage with him, you cannot go back to a philosophy of "ignorance is bliss." What do you do with someone who calls you to think better, to be better, to do better, and to desire to serve with the fullness of who you can be?

Often people think it is the words that are the struggle. I think it is the understanding of the deep and layered thinking offered in *The Servant as Leader*. In fact, you can take any piece of this essay and think that you have the whole concept down. No! The thinking here encompasses the mental, the physical, the emotional, and the spiritual, while also addressing the vision-ary, the strategic, the structural, and the actionable. How can we make sense of this? It overwhelms when we want the "quick bul-let point fix." You will have to look elsewhere for that. As I have often said, Greenleaf is not a cheap date! This writing calls us to live lives of wholeness, "lit from within," by serving others as the means to creating a better society. Along the way, we become

140

wiser, our communities become better, our institutions become distinctive places that "enlarge and liberate." Who would want less?

Fortunately, Greenleaf's writings are evergreen. He still holds a vibrant and liberating vision that has not yet come to full fruition. There are many who write about leadership. Even those writers who are not familiar with Greenleaf's work seem to tap into one of his ideas. I call him the umbrella thinker because almost everything else can fit under his umbrella. He got it right then and he remains right now. Love as a leadership imperative: Greenleaf. Treating people well: Greenleaf. Listening in order to serve: Greenleaf. Building institutions that enlarge and liberate: Greenleaf. Ethical decision making: Greenleaf. Work as part of society building: Greenleaf. I could go on.

When I think of when Greenleaf wrote and how his words apply to our world today, I am amazed. He still points the way and highlights not only the personal path but the institutional path as well. If we use his work as a guide, we will surely become more whole people who live lives of meaning in institutions that heal while they do their work, and create more just and caring societies. What an incredible vision!

LARRY: In the years since Greenleaf first published *The Servant as Leader,* many individuals within institutions have adopted servant leadership as a guiding philosophy. Servant leadership has influenced many noted writers, thinkers, and leaders. Max De Pree, former chairman of the Herman Miller Company and author of *Leadership Is an Art* and *Leadership Jazz,* said that "the servanthood of leadership needs to be felt, understood, believed, and practiced." And Peter Senge, author of *The Fifth Discipline,* has said that he tells people "not to bother reading any other book about leadership until you first read Robert Greenleaf's book, *Servant Leadership*. I believe it is the most singular and useful statement on leadership I've come across."

In recent years, a growing number of servant-leaders and readers have "rediscovered" Robert Greenleaf's own writings through books by De Pree, Senge, Covey, Wheatley, Autry, and many other popular writers.

An increasing number of companies have adopted servant leadership as part of their corporate philosophy or as a foundation for their mission statement. Among these are The Toro Company (Minneapolis, Minnesota), Synovus Financial Corporation (Columbus, Georgia), ServiceMaster Company (Downers Grove, Illinois), The Men's Wearhouse (Fremont, California), Southwest Airlines (Dallas, Texas), Starbucks (Seattle, Washington), and TDIndustries (Dallas, Texas).

Interest in the philosophy and practice of servant leadership is now at an all-time high. Thousands of articles on servant leadership have appeared in various magazines, journals, and newspapers over the years. Many books on the general subject of leadership have been published that recommend servant leadership as a more holistic way of serving. And, today there is a growing body of literature available on the understanding and practice of servant leadership. Greenleaf's books and essays have been published in more than a dozen different languages. Likewise, a number of organizations promoting servant leadership have been established in countries around the world.

Life is full of curious and meaningful paradoxes. Servant leadership is one such paradox that has slowly but surely gained countless adherents since 1970. The seeds that have been planted have begun to sprout in many institutions, as well as in the hearts of many who long to improve the human condition. Servant leadership, and this essay, provide a framework from which many people are helping to improve how we serve, then lead, those who do the work within human society. Servant leadership truly offers hope and guidance for a new era in human development, and for the creation of better, more caring institutions.

> **REVIEW QUESTIONS**: Looking back on the full essay, what stands out the most for you? Why? What do you think is the most challenging idea or concept in the essay? Why? What do you plan to do next, as a servant-leader? Why?

§§

About Robert K. Greenleaf

Robert K. Greenleaf (1904-1990)

Robert K. Greenleaf was born and raised in Terre Haute, Indiana. He joined AT&T in 1926 and worked there until his retirement in 1964. Toward the end of his career, he served as AT&T's Director of Management Research. He also held a joint appointment as visiting lecturer at M.I.T.'s Sloan School of Management and at the Harvard Business School, and taught at Dartmouth College and the University of Virginia. After retiring from AT&T in 1964, he served as a consultant for Ohio University, M.I.T., Ford Foundation, R.K. Mellon Foundation, Lilly Endowment and the American Foundation for Management Research.

In 1970, Greenleaf published the first edition of his essay, *The Servant as Leader*, which coined the phrase "servant-leader" and launched the modern servant leadership movement. This was followed by a series of essays and reflections, including *The Institution as Servant, Trustees as Servants, Teacher as Servant,* "Servant Leadership in Business," "Servant Leadership in Education," "Servant Leadership in Foundations," and "Servant Leadership in Churches." He continued to write and speak until his death in 1990.

About the Contributors

Cheryl Bachelder is the CEO of Popeyes® Louisiana Kitchen, Inc., a multibillion-dollar chain of more than 2,200 restaurants around the world. She has been profiled in the *Wall Street Journal* and the *New York Times*. In 2012, she was recognized as Leader of the Year by the Women's Foodservice Forum and received the industry's highest award, the Silver Plate Award, from the International Foodservice Manufacturers Association. Bachelder has enjoyed thirty-five years of leadership at Yum! Brands, Domino's Pizza, RJR Nabisco, the Gillette Company, and Procter & Gamble. She serves on the board of Pier 1 Imports.

Linda W. Belton served as a Senior Executive in the Veterans Health Administration as Director, Veterans Integrated Service Network (1995-2008), and Director of Organizational Health/Deputy Director, National Center for Organization Development (2008-2015). She received three Presidential Rank awards for her professional contributions. Previously, she administered the Wisconsin State Hospital system (1987-1995), and served in executive leadership positions in private sector health care organizations.

Belton holds an RN from Jameson Memorial Hospital School of Nursing, a B.S. from the University of the State of New York, and an MS from Columbia Pacific University. She was a Johnson Fellow at the Harvard University John F. Kennedy School of Government's program for Senior Executives in State and Local Government, and completed the University of Rochester's program, Leading Organizations to Health. She is the author of *A Nobler Side of Leadership: The Art of Humanagement—A Servant Leader Journey* (Greenleaf, 2016), and co-authored "Creation of a Multi-Rater Feedback Assessment for the Development of Servant Leaders in the Veterans Health Administration" (*Journal of Servant Leadership: Theory and Practice*, 2015). Belton served on the Board of Trustees of the Greenleaf Center for Servant Leadership (2011-2015), and is an Associate of the Sisters of the Sorrowful Mother. She can be contacted at linda9belton@gmail.com.

Patricia M. Falotico is the CEO of the Robert K. Greenleaf Center for Servant Leadership. Founded in 1964 by Robert Greenleaf, the Center advances the philosophy and practice of servant leadership which enriches individuals, builds better organizations and ultimately creates a better, more caring society. Falotico retired from IBM after thirty-one years leading a broad range of projects including technical sales, sales management, service business development, software distribution, marketing, and development of business partner relationships on the local, regional, national and international level. She served as IBM's Senior State Executive for Georgia and Senior Location Executive for Atlanta, providing leadership for IBM in the community and across the state, linking Corporate Citizenship and Employee Engagement activities with strategic IBM initiatives. She currently chairs the United Way of Greater Atlanta's Community Engagement Council and is an active alumna and volunteer of Leadership Atlanta. She mentors emerging women leaders through Pathbuilders' Achieva program. The Greenleaf Center website is www.greenleaf.org. Patricia can be contacted at pfalotico@greenleaf.org.

Don M. Frick is a university professor, keynote speaker, workshop leader, and expert in how organizations implement servant leadership. He is the author of *Implementing Servant Leadership: Stories from the Field; Greenleaf and Servant-Leader Listening;* and Greenleaf's authorized biography, *Robert K. Greenleaf: A Life of Servant Leadership.* He is co-author with James Sipe of the best-selling *Seven Pillars of Servant Leadership: The Wisdom of Leading by Serving.* Don earned a Master of Divinity degree from Christian Theological Seminary and a PhD in leadership and organizational studies from The Union Institute and University. He has served as a media producer with over 250 radio, television, and corporate scripts to his credit. His email is don@donfrick.com.

Kent M. Keith has been an attorney, state government official, high tech park developer, YMCA executive, and president of two private universities. From 2007 to 2012 he served as CEO of the Greenleaf Center for Servant Leadership in the United States, and from 2012 to 2015 he served as the CEO of the Greenleaf Centre for Servant Leadership (Asia) in Singapore. Kent earned a BA from Harvard University, an MA from Oxford University, a Certificate in Japanese from Waseda University in Japan, a JD from the University of Hawaii, and an EdD from the University of Southern California. He is a Rhodes Scholar. He has given more than a thousand speeches, workshops, and conference papers in the United States and eleven countries in Europe, Asia, and Africa. Articles about him have appeared on the front page of *The New York Times* and in *People* magazine, *The Washington Post*, and *The San Francisco Chronicle.* He is the author of the best-seller, *The Case for Servant Leadership*, as well as *Servant Leadership in the Boardroom: Fulfilling the Public Trust; Questions* *and Answers about Servant Leadership;* and *The Christian Leader at Work: Serving by Leading.* In addition to his servant leadership publications, he is known throughout the world as the author of the Paradoxical Commandments, which were part of a book for student leaders that he wrote in 1968 when he was a college sophomore. His book, *Anyway: The Paradoxical Commandments,* which he published in 2002, became a national best seller and was translated into 17 languages. More than 200,000 copies of his servant leadership and Paradoxical Commandments books have been sold worldwide. His servant leadership websites are www.toservefirst.com and christianleaderatwork.com. He can be reached at drkentkeith@hotmail.com.

Isabel Lopez heads Lopez Leadership Services, a Littleton, Colorado-based company that brings a strong results orientation to leadership development programs for a broad range of clients. A former executive with an extensive background in management and human resources at a Fortune 500 telecommunications company, Isabel has supervised hundreds of people and managed multi-million-dollar budgets. She is a skilled executive coach grounded in the practicalities of organizations where she has both supervised and coached executives. Her formal education is in business administration. Her experience includes marketing, strategic planning, operations, employee assessment, quality measurements, labor relations, supervision, management training, and organizational development. Isabel is known as a provocative weaver of tales and texts. She is a writer who has been published in both business and general interest journals. She is also a contributing author to the books, *Reflections on Leadership* and *Faith in Leadership.* She has most recently authored *The Wisdom of Servant Leadership,* an essay published by the Greenleaf

Center. She has deep experience in leadership development and has been a lead facilitator for many national leadership institutes. Her long association with the Greenleaf Center includes presentations at many levels about *The Servant as Leader*, a philosophy to which she remains deeply committed. Isabel can be reached at Lopez Leadership Services, 720-283-9413, Isabel@ lopezleadership.com

Larry C. Spears is President and CEO of the Larry C. Spears Center for Servant-Leadership, Inc. (Indianapolis), established in 2008. He also serves as Servant-Leadership Scholar at Gonzaga University (Spokane), where he designs and teaches several popular graduate courses including Servant-Leadership and Listen/Discern/Decide. From 1990-2007 he served as President and CEO of the Robert K. Greenleaf Center for Servant Leadership. Spears is a writer and editor who has published hundreds of articles, essays, newsletters, books and other publications on servant leadership. He has been interviewed by dozens of newspapers and journals. A 2004 television broadcast interview of Spears by Stone Phillips on NBC's Dateline was seen by 10 million viewers. He is an editor, contributing author, and creative force behind fifteen books on servant leadership, including *Conversations on Servant-Leadership* (2015), *Practicing Servant-Leadership* (2004), and *Insights on Leadership* (1998). He edited or co-edited all five books of Robert K. Greenleaf's writings that are now in print. Larry has also contributed chapters to a dozen additional books edited by others, including *The Jossey-Bass Reader on Nonprofit and Public Leadership* (2010). He is Series Editor of the Servant-Leadership Essay Series (21 essays; 1999-present), and he serves as the Senior Advisory Editor for *The International Journal of Servant-Leadership* (2005-present). Spears is a frequent speaker on servant leadership. The Spears Center for Servant-Leadership (www.spearscenter.org) is committed to enhancing the global understanding and practice of servant leadership. Larry can be contacted at lspears@spearscenter.org.

Duane Trammell is President of Trammell McGee-Cooper and Associates, Inc., and was a business partner of Dr. Ann McGee-Cooper for thirty-five years until her passing in 2016. Ann was mentored by Robert Greenleaf and discussed *The Servant as Leader* on many occasions. Duane enjoys writing, researching, and developing materials on servant leadership. He has co-authored *Time Management for Unmanageable People, You Don't Have To Go Home from Work Exhausted!, Being the Change: Profiles from Our Servant Leadership Learning Community*, and *Awakening Your Sleeping Genius: A Journaling Approach to Servant Leadership*. Duane recently published *The Art of Coaching for Servant Leadership* that he co-authored with Deborah Welch and Ann McGee-Cooper. As a business educator and leadership development specialist, Duane's specialty is designing and delivering participant-based learning. Educational awards have included "Dallas Teacher of the Year" and being named as "One of Three Outstanding Teachers in Texas." He also recently received CoreNet's 2016 Industry Excellence Award—Leadership Development for the project team that built the New Parkland Hospital, a 1.3 billion-dollar project in Dallas, Texas.

About the Greenleaf Center for Servant Leadership

The Greenleaf Center was founded by Robert K. Greenleaf in 1964 as the Center for Applied Ethics, Inc. The Center was renamed the Robert K. Greenleaf Center in 1985, and does business today as the Greenleaf Center for Servant Leadership. The Center's mission is to promote the awareness and practice of servant leadership throughout the world. For more information, please contact:

The Greenleaf Center for Servant Leadership

133 Peachtree Street, NE
Lobby Suite 350
Atlanta, GA 30303

Phone: 404-836-0126
Fax 404-836-01328
www.greenleaf.org

Made in the USA
Lexington, KY
01 August 2017